FOOTLOOSE
& FANCY-FREE

by GLADYS BENNETT

The Bracebridge Examiner Limited
Bracebridge, Ontario

Bennett, Gladys, 1901-
Footloose & Fancy-Free

Collection of author's columns from
the Bracebridge Examiner, 1981-1996
ISBN 0-9697916-1-5

I. Bracebridge Examiner
II. Title.
III. Title: Footloose and fancy-free

PN4913.B32A3 1997   C818'.5403 C97-900255-9

Edited by Susan Pryke

Published by:
THE BRACEBRIDGE EXAMINER LIMITED
16 Manitoba Street,
P.O. Box 1049
Bracebridge, Ontario
P1L 1V2

Dedication

This book, such as it is, is dedicated
to my sister Ethel — "Thel" — always richly
companionable during many long years
sharing youthful sports, all sorts of music,
world travel, the quiet joys of home life.

YOUNG TRAVELLERS: Gladys Bennett (standing) and her sister Thel pose for a picture in Bermuda in 1920, en route to the West Indies.

Contents

Who do we know so much alive
As Gladys Bennett at 95?
She travels to the farthest climes
Then chronicles her life and times
What shall we wish for Gladys B?
Health, honours and felicity!

George and Marilyn James
on the occasion of Gladys Bennett's
95th birthday, June 23, 1996

Foreword

Many will regard Gladys Bennett as a teacher, an entertainer, an activist, or a friend, but to me she is first and foremost a blithe spirit — a rare individual who electrifies the air around her.

Life, for Gladys, is a grand adventure, to be savoured with gusto and good humour. She climbed the Great Wall of China, lost her way on the subways in Russia, and hiked across Scotland in the driving rain — all at an age when most of her contemporaries were thinking about putting a down payment on a sturdy rocking chair. At 95 years of age, Gladys is now making plans for a trip to Guyana, one of the poorest of the Third World countries.

Travel is not only a pleasure, but a purpose for Gladys: she is on a fact-finding mission, of sorts, gleaning information to share with others when she returns. In this way she hopes to improve international relations amongst the citizens of the world. Gladys took her first trip at the age of two, when her mother and father emigrated to Canada. Gladys was born in London, England in 1901, the daughter of Arthur and Marion Bennett. She had three brothers (Harold, Percy and Stanley) and a sister Ethel, who became a perfect companion both at home and when travelling.

By the time they'd reached their teenage years, the girls had become seasoned travellers having taken many trips with their parents to Europe and the United States, never knowing where, exactly, they'd be bedding down each night. Gladys was in Grade 11 when the family struck out across the globe. She took her school books with her and studied each night, determined she would have the credits she'd need to get her university education.

She aspired to attend University of Toronto, as her brothers Harold and Percy before her. She graduated with an honours degree in History and English from Victoria College in 1925 and became a teacher. She taught for more than 30 years, retiring in 1962 as head of the English department at York Memorial Collegiate Institute in Toronto. It was when she was still teaching that Gladys took on the world in earnest, striking further afield to Mexico, Japan and India.

Gladys and Ethel retired to Bracebridge, having been charmed by the locale when they vacationed at High Falls in the 1950s. Here, they took an active role in community life, directing and staging plays and musical entertainment, also playing their part in the Cancer Society and Meals on Wheels. From Bracebridge they made frequent trips to countries in every continent: Asia, South America, Africa, as well as to Europe and to other parts of North America (like Alaska), and, of course, to Australia and New Zealand.

Once they'd experienced various cultures and climes, they felt compelled to share the experience with others in hopes that people might grow more tolerant and learn that the world is, as Gladys puts it, "a planet, not a country."

To that end, the sisters began putting together comprehensive and entertaining travelogues on their various adventures. Ethel died in 1991, but Gladys has continued to travel, on her own.

The popularity of the travelogues both in Bracebridge and

further afield, proved that Gladys was an excellent storyteller. It is no surprise, then, that she was asked to write a column in the Bracebridge Examiner, appropriately titled "Footloose and Fancy-Free".

What follows here is a collection of some of the best of Gladys Bennett's columns, written between the years 1981 and 1996. They run the gamut from serious contemplation of the issues and events of the day, to humorous revelations on life, often inspired by her fascination with the world of nature.

There is a timeless quality to Gladys' writing. Like gems in a jewel box, her stories will sparkle in the light each time you open the cover.

Susan Pryke

Chapter One:
Nature

Dandelions and trilliums

I'm not sure what sense you'll be able to make of that heading up there other than it's something about flowers. You may go on, as I did, to classify the dandelions as commonplace and the trilliums as exceptional — or speaking in human terms, the plebes versus the aristocrats. It's a fact, I think, that we tend to downgrade the dandelion and elevate the trillium into a sort of VIP status. Just how did this come to pass, and is it merited or wise?

Well, certainly the dandelion blooms everywhere — on the roadsides, on our lawns, etc., whereas the trillium, generally speaking, keeps itself aloof in the relative seclusion of the shady woods. However, it's not so snobbish as to scorn completely the edge of a road if conditions there are sufficiently to its liking. But the dandelion, on the other hand, is the least discriminatory, or choosey, of all our Ontario wildflowers. Here, it says to itself, is a patch of ground, let's populate it!

And so we see these great clumps of dandelions growing together cozily, in families of tens and dozens, all along our highways and byways, quite indifferent to the dust being showered by the passing traffic on their golden heads. It's quite otherwise with the trilliums who scatter themselves widely throughout the quiet woods, keeping neat, decent spaces between their aristocratic, pure-white blooms. Dandelions, we see, are ready to take any ground that's handy and available, while trilliums are definitely selective.

Does this difference apply all up and down the created world? From the lowest to the highest creations? (If we dare to make such distinctions.) Well, so far as I've observed them, human beings want the best of both conditions, the close-knit community of the dandelion and the individual aloneness of the trillium. We want to work and play together (because then we can share our burdens?), but at the same time we crave privacy (because we want to keep our best ideas to ourselves?).

Springtime music is a joyful noise

It was Bliss Carman, I think, who described the springtime chorus of the frogs with that poetic word "pandean." Pan, you may remember, was the Greek god who played his pipes so entrancingly, that he made a name for himself as the pre-eminent musician of the natural world. So it's not out of place to invoke his name now when the air all around us these days is full of springtime music.

It was the frogs in our swamp up Lone Pine Drive which first reminded me of Carman's phrase "chorus pandean" (I hope I've got it right) because they were piping at the top of their excited voices. I'm not sure that their concerted noise is melodious enough to be called music, but then, of course, much disharmony and even raucousness is accounted acceptable nowadays in the musical world. Anyway, the frogs seemed to be having a lovely time of it in the warming water, and we passersby naturally shared their exuberance, regardless of any finer points of musical tonality.

Then there are the robins. We have at least three pairs of them here in this vicinity, and at times all the males demonstrate their vocal prowess and expertise in loud, ecstatic song. I'm still trying to puzzle out whether they're singing in harmony or counterpoint, probably the latter as the melody lines overtake one another, and then go madly off into individual improvisations.

There are other singers joining this pandean chorus, of course; the song sparrows and the purple finches, for instance. But these little vocalists seem to aim at refinement rather than noisy exuberance, content to warble a few nicely turned cadences then fly off about their business of territorial and nesting-site claims. I've nothing against volume and choral singing, but one's ears do at times protest "Enough!" when the musicians gang up in this springtime frenzy of the frogs and robins.

I'm not sure that I'm being fair when I introduce percussion into a pandean chorus, but I can't resist mentioning the steady rat-a-tat-tat rhythm of the flickers and other peckers in the woods these days, or maybe on the telephone poles along our streets.

Because it's part of my personality to be rather light-hearted, I usually talk about the natural world as though it were mostly just a pleasant and lovable place. But beneath this surface of casual appreciation, I hope that you'll sense from time to time a deep concern on my part, an attitude which approaches awe. There is nothing trivial, even pleasantly trivial, about the birds and their songs, for instance. Everything in nature, so it seems to me, shows forth the glory of God, and therefore our response to it should be a feeling of awe as well as delight.

...Nature never did betray...

You'll likely agree that this heading has a sort of unfinished look. Indeed, what's the business of betrayal got to do with nature? One thinks of people betraying each other, and a nasty sort of business it is. But nature? How could the woods and streams, the flowers and birds, the earth and sky, how could any of them be thought to betray us? Well, of course, the poet, William Bryant who wrote these words, was making the point that those who love nature can always depend on it when they need it.

Of course, there are all too many natural disasters — earthquakes, floods, cyclones, etc. Yes, they may cause destruction and even death, but I still don't think that we can rightfully accuse them of betrayal; that's to say, of a breach of faith.

So far as I know, the forces of nature have never promised or guaranteed us earthlings security and ease. If you like to take the story of the expulsion from the Garden of Eden as an explanation of our human insecurity, that's one way of looking at our trials and tribulations. But for myself, all my long life through, guilty or not of manifold sins, I've found the beauties and wonders of nature to be my ever true-and-faithful friends.

One could give countless instances. It seems to me that whenever I've felt in need of comfort, I've found it by getting outdoors. Then, almost at once, there's a flower in bloom, or a butterfly on the wing, a rippling stream, or a surging ocean. In the wintertime there's the cold, blue-green magic of snow and ice. You will see from all these examples (and many more which are even now on the tip of my pen) that nature has never betrayed at least one of its life-long lovers!

Even now, as I write, my spirits are revived as I watch the chickadees and goldfinches flitting to and fro as they visit the bird feeders hanging out there on the clothesline. But how about the less welcome pigeons? Well, surely they, too, bring joy to the hearts of children when they come and perch fearlessly on shoulders, on hands, and even on heads!

And what if you do find yourself walking in the rain? Isn't there a song that tells us how delightful that can be (especially if you are in love — with a girl, or just with life itself). And if you're caught in a veritable downpour, doesn't it often serve to wash away your anxieties and self-pity? (Of course, it's a good idea to have an umbrella with you and hope that it won't be blown inside-out by a playful gust of wind.)

After reading all this, you'll see how I'm determined to prove my case; namely, that nature will never leave us uncomforted in times of need. I grant the natural disasters, but maintain, rather stubbornly, that they are not only incidental, and not nearly so terrible and terrifying, spiritually speaking, as the selfish cruelty of many human beings.

In conclusion, I might suggest that some of us who have the

means, the imagination, and the goodwill might play our part in helping the deserts bloom with roses, and the barren rocks gush forth clean, sparkling water.

An apology for Bertram and Prissy

It's about time, I think, to return to my favourite subject, namely the birds who come to our back-garden feeder.

This feeding station of ours is all of seven or eight feet long, part of the old stone foundation wall of a former house. As a consequence of its unusual length we can accommodate, simultaneously, the descent of a dozen or so sparrows, several blue jays, a flock of voracious grosbeaks, as well as other occasional guests like the nuthatches and woodpeckers. Besides these there are, of course, the chickadees, and last but far from least, the mourning doves. It is about the doves that I feel constrained to write at greater length.

One might think that all doves would feel a certain commitment to peace, or at the very least, to a sort of non-aggressive tolerance. But it's not so with our Bertram the Bully. (Don't ask me how he got his name; it's one of those things which just happen.) Bertram seems never to have heard of laissez-faire, nor has he ever considered such a feeble philosophy as live-and-let-live. No! Bertram challenges every comer to the banquet table (except perhaps the squirrels). He obviously believes in, and acts upon, the Darwinian theory of the-survival-of-the-fittest. My sister and I are fairly good at chasing off cats (and even the squirrels), but Bertram merely circles the garden, perches, pro tem, in a tree, and then returns directly our backs are turned and we have retreated indoors. It's very discouraging when you have a greedy, boorish bully like Bertram.

Then there's a tree sparrow of a similarly pugnacious, cantankerous disposition. So far we haven't a clue as to the sex of either Bertram or this nasty little sparrow, but since we've dubbed the dove a male, we'll divide the honours equally and call the sparrow Peckin' Prissy. She looks modest enough to be a Prissy, but her manners are bold and shocking, and so, we presume, are her ethics. Once she's taken up her position on the table, she also challenges all later arrivals. It's not a pretty sight, especially on the very Eve of Christmas. Prissy, no doubt, believes in that facile, quasi-religious motto stated as "The Lord helps those who help themselves," even though it takes a few pecks here and there.

However, since such oafish, belligerent doves and sparrows have not, so far, caused nearly so much damage in the world as we humans, I've learnt to fuss and fume quietly in private while continuing to spread out the daily seeds for all who come to the table. Perhaps both Bertram and Prissy will appreciate my forbearance, even though given so grudgingly, and mend their anti-social ways.

Groundhogs, beavers, et al

While other people have cats and dogs wandering around in their gardens, we have a couple of groundhogs. In the nature of things, I shouldn't be surprised if this turns into a happy family with the addition of several little ground-piglets.

Then, in our swamp up Naismith Road we have beavers. Neither of these furry creatures, groundhogs nor beavers, is exactly the stuff of poetry, though the beaver has got himself a place of honour as our national emblem as well as providing the motif for one side of the lowly nickel.

This story, then, is in the nature of an appreciation, an apology, or at least a gracious acceptance of such unromantic creatures as these. And so it will include, too, passing references to the raccoons, squirrels, chipmunks, and perhaps even a distant look at the gophers out West.

When the groundhogs took up residence, summer and winter, beneath our shed, I made inquiries as to whether they presented any danger to us humans including our neighbours' children. No, was the reply, but they will help themselves to any young vegetables in your garden-plots. Since all of us now seem to have grown too sophisticated, busy, or lazy to grow our own vegetables, the groundhogs have been allowed to settle in comfortably and permanently. They keep a wary eye on us, and we do likewise on them. So far, unlike the more handsome raccoons, they don't seem to covet the leftovers in our garbage bags, which gives them the status of good neighbourliness.

When it comes to assessing the pros and cons in regard to the beavers in the swamp, we have to think again. Although they would seem to pose no threat to human or other animal life, they certainly do wreak havoc on the poplars. All along the edges of the swamp they have gnawed their busy incisors through trunk after trunk so that the hillsides are littered with fallen, half-stripped trees.

About ten years ago these beavers became so numerous and destructive that I gave the word to a local trapper to go and catch some of them. Mind you, I didn't want them eliminated, exterminated, or anything so drastic, but it seemed necessary to curb their activities, to place a limit on their "busyness." Now, when I walk beside the swamp, two of the remaining inhabitants swim quite close to shore, whack the water resoundingly, dive under, make a short circuit, and repeat the performance to stake their claim and give me a warning.

When one recalls how greatly in earlier times the beaver contributed to the wealth of our pioneer forbears as well as to the native peoples, we most certainly can't damn them out of their Canadian existence. They still stand as the symbol of our industry, besides having provided an aristocratic title for a famous Canadian, namely, Lord Beaverbrook.

So far as I can recall, the whole tribe of squirrels — black, grey and red — have done nothing much to endear themselves to their human fellows, except whisk their tails and make Tarzan-like leaps, which do elicit a fair degree of admiration. But the way in which the big black ones gobble up and carry off the sunflower seeds certainly elicits feelings of a very different sort. Nonetheless, I'll admit that their waggish insouciance does have a kind of charm. However, when we move on to a consideration of the pretty little chipmunks, we find ourselves simply oozing tenderness.

Laughing at the moon

Laughter strikes me as being a very rare commodity these days. Giggles arise often among the young crowd, and smirks and their ilk are common enough, but honest-to-goodness laughter seems to be sadly out of style. And I can't claim to be anything special at it myself, although I'm usually capable of wearing a smile of sorts.

It was in the Boston Museum of Fine Art that I chanced upon a Chinese scroll which showed a Buddhist priest looking up at the full moon and obviously laughing with pleasure at the sight. It was a delightful piece of art in the traditional black-and-white brush-work of the Chinese and it tickled my fancy. Perhaps I came upon it at a time when life seemed rather boring or definitely unpleasant; anyway, I have recalled it frequently for more than 30 years, each time with renewed pleasure.

During those years I have looked up at several hundred full moons. Not always with laughter, of course, because sometimes they have been so startlingly beautiful, orange or silver, that I've been too entranced, too awed, to express my pleasure in laughter. Silence held me then.

But I very much like this idea of sharing a joke with nature, whether it's something inanimate like the moon, or lively like the chipmunk. After all, there's no good reason to conclude that Creation is supposed to be a dead-serious affair. Everything hasn't proved itself to be a disaster in the natural world, even though it's almost invariably the earthquake, wind, or fire that gets news coverage.

So, it's nice to think that the robin, though he or she keeps a wary eye on me as I roam the garden, is nevertheless ready to greet me as a kindly neighbour. In fact, I can easily imagine inviting my robins in for an afternoon cup of tea if that were a mutual form of relaxation.

Certainly a great many horticulturists do smile affectionately at the flowers blooming in their gardens.

There is a real personal grief, too, when they find a pansy drooping her head, or a marigold with its stem snapped. Sometimes I wonder, though, whether we take enough time in our task of watering to pause and say thank you to all these bright summer visitors in our gardens. Perhaps it's just as much of an effort for them to keep putting on a brave face on things as it is for us!

It's mostly for the birds

Many of you will have discovered that, for better or worse, I am essentially a nature lover, with a special weakness for birds. You won't be surprised, then, by this article's heading, and I trust that you won't be annoyed either since I have two or three (or four or five) comments about birds on the very tip of my pencil, along with a couple of stories to tell.

So far in my various observations I can't recall having drawn your attention to the vociferous twanging of the purple martins as they wheel around their many-nested house over the old post office building. They may have been encouraged to return there each year in order to keep down the mosquito population, but actually it's the music of their airy guitars which most of us note with amusement and joy.

Then, you've probably encountered lately, as I have, those road-addicted grouse who pause two or three feet from the verge, teasing you into jamming your brakes, or swerving over the centre line. That's not to forget, either, the ubiquitous low-flying robins who seem to take a special delight in a last-second dash across to their nests or their offspring on the opposite side of the road.

The ingenuity of some small birds constantly amazes me. For instance, feature the smartness of the sparrow who lands neatly on the slender stem of a blade of tufted grass in order to weigh it down so that it can pick out the seeds. Is this skill instinctive, handed down through countless generations of sparrows, or is this particular bird capable of thinking things out and mastering a new technique?

One of the funniest sights I've ever seen was that of a vireo tugging out a long slug of some sort from the bark of a wild cherry tree; having stretched it along a firm branch, he (or she) began to smash and mash it into the right consistency for safe mastication. I was reminded of the tit-willow lyric in the "The Mikado" where the singer suggests that the melancholy song of the tit was the result of having "a rather tough worm in his little inside."

Let's be fair (to chickens)

A week or so ago, I finished an article with the familiar expression "Smell a rat." Now I feel that I owe an apology to all rats as well as to a number of other animals. We human beings have been all too ready to denigrate our fellow creatures like the rat, the wolf, the pig, the chicken,... well, you can add several others of your own choosing. For a moment I'm going to return to the chicken or its mother, the hen.

Why is it that we almost always seize on the actions of some species of animal in order to describe our own failure? Why do we use expressions like "chicken-out" when we want to explain our own lack of courage? None of us has yet entered into the heart or brain or instinct of a chicken to know whether its seeming timidity is to be reckoned as good or bad. Hens and chicks have survived remarkably well in the wilds as in our farmyards. Moreover, we owe to them, in the wilds as much as in captivity, a food considered almost irreplaceable. If they hesitate to encounter the wheels of a moving car, or if they become confused in their sudden realization of danger, how can we humans assess the weakness or wisdom of such behaviour?

Perhaps I'm particularly indignant about the phrase "chickening-out" because it has been applied specifically to a certain point in the ascent of Ayers Rock in Australia. It's my own strong feeling that the Rock (since it has long been regarded as sacred by the aborigines) shouldn't be climbed by Whites at all. But if their ego demands that they attempt to scramble to its top, and then find themselves unable to proceed for one cause or another, let them acknowledge their own weakness in turning back in strictly human terms, such as shortness of breath, dizziness, or an inability to find secure footing.

All of these difficulties could be labelled as cowardice, I suppose, but far more fairly we should accept them as wisdom. To push a human into taking unnecessary risks is to behave like a fool, which is quite a different matter from acting like a chicken in quite different circumstances.

As I mentioned above, there is a whole dictionary of such

terms as "chickening-out," and at a later date I may return to the topic and inveigh against some more of them, because I feel so strongly about this unfair practice of ours in holding animals up to scorn by indirectly ascribing to them our own human weaknesses — weaknesses like indecision, gluttony, ruthlessness, and so on, almost indefinitely.

In conclusion, and since I happen to be writing this on a Sunday, it would be nice to remind you how Jesus is said to have wept over Jerusalem, and to have exclaimed how he would have gathered its people together into safety as the mother hen gathers her chicks under her protective wings.

Little leaf, little planet

There's a negro spiritual which talks about the "little, tiny baby" being in the hands of God, and then goes on to include the "big, wide world." But recently I've been struck with the thought that the world, too, might better be described in such words as "this tiny, little planet." We are becoming increasingly aware these days of the smallness of the earth as it wends its infinitesimal way in the immensity of the universe.

During the millennia of man's consciousness of the whirling systems all around him, perhaps there was a time when he had good reason to think that this tiny planet was the centre of creation and perhaps it is! No dogmatic yes or no can be said to that!

But my theme for this week's article is simply the importance of littleness, whether it's a tiny green leaf on a burgeoning tree, or the tiny grain of matter which we call the Earth.

Why do our hearts grow warm and tender within us when we look all around us these May days, and see those fragile little leaves venturing out bright and sticky with new life? Do we admire their courage as well as recognize their vulnerability? In the past, many of us have winced with a sort of fellow-suffering when we have seen them withering and dying from the spray of some defoliant — even when our notions of human progress have called for their destruction. But now we are considering the fate, not only of the tiny leaf, but also of our similarly tiny planet.

I'm all in favour of the exploration of the farthermost spaces. I can't imagine a human race which doesn't go venturing into every conceivable unknown place, whether here on earth or beyond the present reach of telescope or mind. But what if, after all, this planet is our only "home"? Are we appreciative enough of its vulnerability? Of its dependence upon us humans to tend and keep it safe and green?

There's rightly real distress among many of us when we realize the too frequent failure of adults to provide the world's little children with all that their health and happiness requires. There's a telling phrase which goes "the child of a feckless family." The child, by a stretch of the imagination, could well refer to our young planet, and we human beings its feckless family. It's not easy to define that word feckless, but if we consider for a moment our present thoughtlessness, carelessness, neglect, and crass stupidity about our environment, we may approach some understanding of it.

So I return to a rather perturbed consideration of the tiny green leaf, the tiny little baby, and our tiny fragile planet — all so dependent upon us to act as the agent of the hand of God to protect and hold them safe.

The role of the wilderness

Always there's a debate going on nowadays as to whether or not certain parts of the earth should remain uncultivated, left as wilderness areas. We've already cleared and cultivated so much of the planet that our environmentalists are vigorously crusading to prevent any further "damage." So what is the case for preserving all wilderness — forest, bush, and desert?

Actually, my chief concern here is not so much about keeping the land uncultivated as keeping it uninhabited, free from all the clutter and trappings of civilization. A place, that is, of undisturbed quiet where one can go, be alone, and take stock of things. To withdraw, voluntarily, into isolation, and so escape for a time, at least, the confusion and pressures of life — that's the hope of many a weary and worldly heart. The monks and nuns in the Middle Ages sought in monasteries and convents all over Europe just this sort of sanctuary in order to work, write, and pray. And we in our own difficult times need to find similar places for the refreshment and renewal of our spirits.

The Bible gives two good examples of time being well spent in the wilderness: First, when the Israelites were making their journey from slavery to freedom; and secondly, when Jesus withdrew for those forty days alone in the desert while he deliberated upon the way in which his earthly mission should be carried out. In both instances the isolation in the wilderness would seem to have been a time of spiritual growth.

But to find such a wilderness close at hand is difficult, as we well know here in Muskoka. No longer do we readily find it beside our lakes and in our forests, which not so long ago provided a sanctuary from urban stress. Our resorts are now largely places of recreational hustle and bustle! They have their delights to offer, but not the quiet wilderness for which we must always search.

But let's not too quickly and easily despair! After all, most of us do know a quiet lakeside or roadside spot where we can go apart, and in a comparative silence, relax and think about the things of the spirit. Probably there will still be the hum of traffic in the distance, but it need not disturb our mood anymore than the twittering of the birds, or the sound of the wind in the trees. Perhaps we can even find a room in the house where the babble of voices is muted to a murmur.

Of course, there's another, quite different side to this wilderness theme. I'm sure that some of you have already recalled Isaiah's prophecy about the desert blossoming like a rose (and how welcome that would be in many parts of Africa). And if, by any chance, you are familiar with Omar Khayyam's poem "The Rubaiyat," you'll remember that his solitude was shared with his love beside him "singing in the wilderness" (along with the company of a book of verses and a jug of wine)!

Which makes a rather nice conclusion, doesn't it? That we can share our wilderness with those who are dear to us. But that calls for an entirely different article about learning to live wisely and happily with everyone else. As John Donne put it, none of us is an island, desert or idyllic, but all are part of the mainland of our common humanity.

The distant view

Now that the leaves have mostly fallen from the trees and bushes, one gets surprisingly long views into the depths of the woods. Now one can see those scattered rocks jutting up, gray with lichens, green with moss. Through the tracery of bare branches there come glimpses of the sky, pale blue or flushed with sunset. These late autumnal days with their wide and distant views are part of the beauty-cycle we enjoy here in Muskoka.

There are very few, surely, who do not thrill to a wide expanse of sky, of fields, of sea, of lakes like the Great Lakes. After being enclosed within some relatively small space, say a walled room, a city street, or even a garden full of trees and flowers, what a feeling of release it gives to look through uncluttered space to a far horizon! One of my happiest memories of Calgary is the view we used to get of the snow-capped mountains as we emerged from our high school on Crescent Heights. Eighty miles distant, and only all that lovely clean air between our stuffy classrooms and those dazzling peaks!

The appeal of the distant view doesn't necessarily mean that we find no joy in what is close at hand. It's just that the human spirit must feel free to break away occasionally from any form of confinement. Even the most dearly loved home can sometimes become rather like a prison cell.

And in much the same way, even a congenial occupation, and a pleasant social round can seem to confine one into too small, too cramped a box. That is why some of us (and I would correct that to read "a great many of us") feel the need to keep seeking wider horizons. The familiar saying that faraway fields look greener implies that one should be content to "stay put" instead of traipsing off to some distant land or of venturing into some new line of thought. But I still maintain (as one of Canada's footloosiest persons) that without the urge to break free from old narrow bounds, whether physical or mental, life could prove singularly boring, even deadly. And, as I conclude, you may recall that all this moralizing and philosophy arose simply because the leaves have fallen!

Needed: breaths of fresh air

There are at least two fairly obvious ways of talking about fresh air, and you'll not be surprised when I describe them as the literal and the metaphorical. But since I'm not sure which of the two I feel most strongly about at the moment, the course of this article is not yet determined.

I'm inclined to think, however, that it's always easier to begin with facts rather than with fancies, and so I'm dealing first with the very air we breathe, good or bad.

Really pure, fresh air is, unfortunately, unknown to most of us, even in a comparatively underpopulated, unindustrialized country like Canada.

Of course, we still have plenty of pollution from cars, etc., and even right here at home in Bracebridge we have a factory which has had to be warned many times about emitting some rather nasty, smelly gas. And so when I speak about "fresh air" it is of necessity relative to our present unsatisfactory state of affairs.

It's during these winter months, mainly, that the longing for a good breath of fresh air hits the hardest. Because of the cold outside, we all feel the need for warm, cozy rooms in which to relax. But then, because of the high cost of fuel, we tend to seal tight our houses into stuffy pockets of very stale air.

It's true that some hardy and/or extravagant souls fling open windows from time to time, but most of us begrudge the cost of such a solution. Besides which, an open vent always seems to bring a chilly draught down someone's neck and shoulders, and so we hurriedly seal it off.

So, for myself, after a few hours spent cooped up indoors, I find it necessary to drag on all those clumsy outdoor clothes and venture forth. And ah! That first welcome sniff of cold, fresh air!

I sigh with relief and take long breaths to savour it. And it's much the same thing when one leaves a crowded hall or theatre where the atmosphere has become overwarm, even oppressive. Though most of us wouldn't willingly settle for less warmth, at the same time we do relish that breath of fresh air!

Speaking now in metaphorical terms. What is it that most quickly puts us to sleep (again, literally and metaphorically)? To a large extent it's a staleness in our day-to-day lives which induces a state of dozy boredom.

Far too often we've got nothing new and fresh to keep us alert. Everything becomes so routine, so predictable, so warm and cozy, that it's no wonder we grow drowsy and dopey.

Personally, as many of you already know, I've sought much of my own "fresh air" by travelling to countries different from ours here in Canada. Although the actual air in them may at times be warm and sticky, and really quite oppressive, I've usually found that the scenes and situations there have brought many new sights and fresh insights. It's the kind of fresh air which stimulates the mind and wards off the drowsiness of the spirit!

Others of you, I'm sure, have found other ways of getting it

— that breath of fresh air, I mean. Perhaps if you're still young and robust, it's by taking a brisk walk in our winter wonderland, or by skimming down a hill or two on your skis.

But as the body rejoices, don't forget that minds and spirits also have their claims, and for the human race they must surely be held as its ultimate destiny.

Enjoying the sound of the crunching snow

I can't say that I'm a one hundred per cent enthusiast when it comes to snow. As the flakes pile up and up, through the centimetres into the metres along my driveway, I admit to hoping for a gentle thaw. But on the pro-side of the matter, there's nothing, I'd maintain, quite so exhilarating and musical as the crunch of snow beneath one's feet. That sound gives a boost to one's spirits with which few others can compare or compete.

It may, of course, be the combination of several weather-factors that is responsible for the crunching and the resulting exhilaration. For instance, the air must be clear as well as cold, and, above all, be comparatively still. A wind definitely discourages any lingering in one's tracks, and has us scurrying as fast as our legs can carry us into the shelter and warmth of the house. Moreover, I doubt that our delight in the crunching sound would be half as great if there weren't, along with it, the sparkle on the snow. (I particularly like the magic of moonlight).

There are, of course, all the strings of coloured lights to add to the excitement. My own small display boasts only a dozen or so bulbs, but my neighbours, up and down the street, have festooned their trees and houses with hundreds of them. Probably the energy-conservationists look with a jaundiced eye at all this Christmas prodigality, but we can come back at them with the well known saying that Christmas comes but once a year. I suppose the ancient Romans celebrated their feast of Saturnalia with flaming torches carried through the streets or fixed into innumerable sconces, and thus were also guilty of damaging the environment.

Glancing out the window as I write, I see the glitter of snowflakes, each catching the sun's sheen as it floats through the air. The flakes are so small that they have no white fluff to them, but are like tiny sequins decorating the winter's party dress. And now, to make things lively as well as lovely, there are three or four chickadees flitting gaily to and fro, breakfasting on sunflower seeds. I have often wondered how the birds keep their tootsies warm when the thermometer drops down to zero as it did this morning. Maybe it's the oil in the seeds which stokes their little furnaces and provides the necessary heat.

From the delights and beauties of nature, it is our fate to return to the complexities of human society. Yet I hesitate to introduce any end-of-the-year, Cassandra-like note of foreboding. Like many other people on this troubled planet, I cherish the hope that all's not yet lost as we prepare to meet the challenge of the unknown 90s ahead of us. Surely there's now sufficient awareness of the dangers threatening the earth to keep the global family from making anymore death-dealing blunders.

At this moment I note that a pair of blue jays has arrived at the feeder and the chickadees have decided that it would be wiser and safer to give way to their superior weight. But from my past observation of nature and history I am still hopeful that the end of the story will prove that the large and the small, the bold and the meek, will be able to find ways of balancing and harmonizing the good things of the earth so as to accommodate everything and everybody on this lovely planet.

Such, anyway, is my hope and prayer as the year ends.

GLADYS BENNETT with the family puppy, Calgary, 1912.

CHAPTER TWO:
IDEAS

Looking back on two World Wars

My memories have to go a long way back to see again any-thing to do with the First World War.

I had barely entered my teens when it began, and had just left high school when it ended. My brothers all enlisted, and so did their friends, but they were considerably older than I.

We at home and in school, we knitted and sewed, and regu-larly posted parcels overseas to soldiers at the front and rela-tives in England.

When peace came in 1918, my parents at once made plans to "go home" to England, and then to cross over to France.

It was my first experience of seeing the devastation caused by war, of seeing cemeteries filled with "row on row" of white crosses as we visited the graves of Calgary boys who had given their lives in those years of bitter warfare.

Like most teenagers, I found the whole thing very shocking, and only vaguely explainable. It was afterwards, in the 1920s, when I studied history at college, that I began to understand how nations could get themselves into such armed confrontations, dying in thousands and millions.

During the next 20 years, I more or less rejected, in my mind at least, the reasonableness or necessity of war.

Undoubtedly, the books I read, like "Goodbye To All That" by Graves, and "Testament of Youth" by Vera Britain, greatly influenced me. And then in 1935-36, while I was teaching in England (on exchange), I was even more affected by the strongly pacifist position of a great many people, as for instance, at Cambridge University.

So we all watched with growing anxiety the rise of Naziism in Germany, and Fascism in Italy. During those mid-thirties it was the British horror at the thought and possibility of another war which led to their policy of appeasement, seen by many as disgraceful, even cowardly!

But, you know as well as I do, that it all began again, the bombs, the suffering, the millions of deaths. And again, here at home in Canada, we Canadians did our knitting and sent our letters and parcels, while our young men again went overseas, often straight out of our high schools, often to their deaths.

And so in 1945, again after long and bitter years of war, came another peace, of sorts. Again our families laid plans to return to England, since my mother longed to see again all our relatives there. But after all, it was I who made the first journey, alone, crossing the Atlantic in a still-unconverted troop-ship, sharing a blacked-out "cabin" with a dozen others — some of whom smoked, nightly, in their berths!

That summer, even in 1949, I found that London was still clearing away the rubble in its bombed sites; it was a London very different from the one I knew in the '30s; in places it was hardly recognizable.

Then I bought a bike, crossed the Channel, and began a long ride through the Netherlands, Belgium and France, returning to England and back to Canada with very mixed feelings.

I suppose I'd become more objective during my own 40s, less apt to rage and weep than when I was a teenager, more saddened than shocked.

Ambitious nations, like many individuals, will act ruthlessly when they think that violence is the quickest, surest way to achieve their "manifest" destinies.

Again, in 1951, I went on my own to Europe, this time travelling mostly on trains and buses, with only a knapsack as a month's luggage. That was still the time of the Allied occupation, and so I fared as a mere civilian in amongst soldiers and their families.

Accordingly, there were times and places when accommodation for visitors like me was precisely nil, and so I was occasionally reduced to spending my nights in railway stations or on trains.

At times I was questioned closely as to why I was there at all! But I got safely down from Holland, through Germany and Austria, and back to England, via the beauty and peace of Switzerland. (And for the first time, I crossed the Atlantic "par avion.")

I'm not quite sure what I wanted to prove or learn by making these two trips to post-war Europe. Certainly, something motivated me beyond mere curiosity. I do wonder at times why it seemed so important to me to share, at least in this small way, the history of 20th century Europe.

For a similar reason I also visited Hiroshima in Japan. Perhaps, in both cases, I was trying to identify myself with the suffering of people elsewhere — while we in North America remained unmolested in our snug homeland.

Personally, I find myself at present with no truly firm commitment to either "peace at any price," or "peace with honour."

But living through two world wars, and sharing the pain of the dozen others waged since the 1940s, I find myself greatly troubled about any resort to violence, even though it be only the throwing of a stone through a window.

To me it seems possible, as well as ethically right, to adjust our desires and ambitions so that no one else suffers while we ourselves prosper, and no one, anywhere, is made to feel expendable in the world into which he has been born.

Dealing with all the loose ends

As I see it, there are two possible ways of dealing with loose ends: either you tie them off, or you splice or knot them, to similar threads. Do you follow me? As an example of the first way, when you've finished knitting a sweater, say, you tie the loose ends. On the other hand, you make a neat join if your thread breaks, or if you come to the untimely end of your ball of wool. So, to repeat, it's tie off, or tie together. However, most of us who have grown old, do nothing much at all, but let the loose ends dangle.

There's a saying that "nature abhors a vacuum," and in a parallel statement it might be said that most humans don't like having any loose ends lying around. We feel uncomfortable and annoyed when we don't finish things off tidily. There's a somewhat similar discomfort when we feel "all tied up in knots," but most of us manage to unravel them, and feel quite pleased at our ingenuity. Of course, sometimes we just hack our way through, much as Alexander the Great did when he cut the Gordion Knot with one sweep of his trusty sword (with no fussing at all about leaving some loose ends).

At times it's fairly easy to ignore any breaks in the continuity of our lives. For instance, when I stopped teaching I'd already made arrangements for travel abroad. In fact, the very summer I retired, I made my first visit to China. So I barely noticed any threads left over from the past but, forthwith, picked up new, exciting, rewarding ones.

However, things are not so easy as one keeps growing older. Nowadays, I have to think twice, or thrice, before starting off for anywhere farther away than Gravenhurst! And frankly, the loose ends of my last trip are still lying all around me as I sort out my colour slides for a show on South Africa.

But here, let's consider other applications of the same thing, that's to say, coping with the loose ends left over from previous, but now discontinued activities. My own devices and methods may not be yours, but here, at least, are a few suggestions. So, as regards to any future travelling, I'll make sure it's relatively effortless, a short, well-conducted tour I've signed up for, or perhaps a "stay-on-the-ship" cruise?

But what about all the more ordinary little loose ends with which we have to deal here at home? When I finish reading this book, must I struggle through snow and ice to the library? No, I can mosey along the old bookcases and pick out something that looks interesting. Ah! here's one on England, with lots of illustration, too!

Other loose ends? My hair straggles and all the ends are split! The floor rugs are frayed and my sweaters are tatty! Well, mostly I just don't bother to deal with such petty things, but move happily from room to room, pausing here to say hello and how are you to an African violet, or a favourite photograph. Then I remember what Shakespeare wrote about sleep knitting up the ravelled sleeve of care, and I put aside all thoughts about dealing with loose ends, big or little, roll myself up in a soft, warm blanket, and snuggle down for a blissful snooze.

Which, possibly, brings us to consider the loose ends of life itself. And again I'm quoting Shakespeare, so wise and serene when he wrote in "The Tempest," that "our little life is rounded with a sleep." For me, that word "rounded" has a very reassuring sound, with no frazzles, no loose ends to spoil my final exit.

Flexibility is the name of the game

When I see the poplar leaves twisting and turning in even the slightest breeze; when I see them dance, each in its own small space, then I feel sure that they're setting me an example of flexibility.

To be flexible means that one is able to move, and no matter how limited, is the sign and meaning of life. The earth and sky are full of it; one might say that there's never a motionless moment. If there were, it would herald the end of things for the planet and everything that's on it. Of course, I'm no scientist, and so I'm making these sweeping statements only in order to further this week's topic. Let's agree, then, that movement is life, and explore for a few paragraphs how and when we move.

Granted, that physical flexibility becomes more and more limited the older we grow. Even those of us who could touch our toes not so long ago wouldn't dare risk it now. Our poor backs have become so stiff that we can hardly move a degree to left or right, and as for that limbo stuff, you can count us out. When we talk about leaning over backwards to please somebody, we must perforce leave any such physical antics to the young limberettes and the ballet dancers of the world.

Yet all of us rightly cling to the essential need for movement, whether of the body or the mind. So long as our knees and fingers don't absolutely refuse to function, we continue to bend and flex them with a certain degree of satisfaction because then we feel we're in harmony with the cloud-flecked, racing sky and the rippling lake. Not even a fine picture of the sky or lake can be truly satisfying unless the artist has captured a feeling of movement.

Probably, though, it is in our minds and wills that flexibility seems so important. Our ability to give and take, to see this as well as that, to come and go lightly with the winds of change, this is the kind of flexibility to which we should aspire if we aim to be the wise children of our Mother Earth.

As we move from summer into autumn, now that August has given way to September, we're all probably taking stock of what change, if any, we might make in our day-to-day activities. There may seem to be little room, or need, to make any drastic changes, but there's every reason that even the most stiff-kneed and stiff-necked among us should aim to do things a little bit better than before.

How do they escape poverty?

How does anyone escape from poverty? That's the persistently nagging question for poor people who are living a hand-to-mouth existence, or are faring even worse.

In earlier times they shifted ground with their herds in search of better grazing, or sailed farther across the seas for fish. But the day came when fixed borders made such free movements impossible or hazardous — guarded by men with loaded guns.

Then what should the poor do? Cross borders illegally if it can't be done legally?

Nowadays, we describe many such impoverished people as belonging to the "Third World."

This classification is based, it seems, on the average income in a country; but to reach such a figure you have to lump together those at the top who are rolling in riches along with the many others who are struggling to survive below a poverty line — whatever that line is reckoned to be!

All of this may sound pretty depressing as a start, but I hope to be neither pessimistic nor critical, but only disturbed by this imbalance in the distribution of the world's wealth.

Like most of you, I feel rather helpless in the face of present conditions as we see them depicted on our TV screens. But at least we can think about them, try to analyze their cause, and even come up with some ideas as to how they might be improved.

But first I'm pointing out two or three of the ways, largely unacceptable to many of us, in which the world's poor go about making their own efforts at improvement. For instance, they batter at the walls of boundaries, practically demanding entry.

My own parents made it into Canada quite legally and comparatively comfortably at the turn of the century; but they were privileged Britons, healthy and far from poor, advantages not shared by the hundreds of thousands who are trying to escape the poverty in their homelands today.

Another way of escape, while still remaining at home in their Third World country, is to ignore any and all standards about pollution. Their industries shock us as they dump chemical waste, etc., into any water that's handy (just as we ourselves have done and continue to do!).

Similarly, they cut down forests and use pesticides (again, just as we've done, and still do). We think, and say loudly, that they should know better, and should either improve their standards, or keep to their old, outmoded ways of farming and manufacture.

Yet another method of escaping poverty is to stop any attempt to change a one-party form of government into a western-style democracy. Praise-worthy as such a change may seem to us, it's almost bound to destablize a developing country as was the case in Russia; and so it was avoided in China.

Stability is the best way to increase trade and commerce, and probably the quickest way to raise the average income in a developing economy. So votes must wait until the Third World status is a thing of the past.

There are, of course, some countries which are ready to fight a war to get what they feel is their right, as Iraq did to get its share of the Persian Gulf oil from the Kuwaiti sheiks. But the war ended with considerable devastation and with no improvement in the Iraqi standard of living.

My own personal drop in the big bucket of economic inequity is mostly to talk and write about it. But I'm making plans to pay a brief visit to Guyana, which is presently rated as one of the poorest of the Third World countries.

Adapt or die!

Have you ever casually tossed off that old saying "do or die?" I can't remember having done so myself, but this week's heading with its change of the word "do" to "adapt" means business, I assure you, even though I may at times treat it lightly.

You see, the important question remains: Are we humans able and willing to adapt our ways of thinking and acting to the changes that are so rapidly going on around us, or are we so smug and/or thick-headed that we'll try to keep things as they are, despite the fact that it might consign us to a dead-end?

I can quote several such alternatives, oft-repeated and almost as disturbing (or meaningless). For instance, there's "sink or swim," "now or never," and "like or lump it." But are we really given a choice in any of them?

The non-swimmer who finds himself in deep water is pretty sure to sink unless someone comes to his rescue. Of course, he should have learned to swim, or worn a life jacket, but since he didn't, poor fellow, he sinks.

If next we consider "now or never," the alternative in actual terms, is just about as meaningless. Here you are, perched on the edge of a major decision: do you or don't you, for instance, risk all your savings in this attractive but unproven enterprise?

Comparatively speaking, our next alternative, "like it or lump it," is less dramatic. Say I'm offered a ride in the back seat of a car when I'd confidently expected to be sharing the front one, there to enjoy the scenery and some pleasant conversation with my driver-friend en route. But now I find that he's got his girlfriend along with him, and he casually relegates me to the non-scenic, non-social back seat of his car! I definitely don't like it, but for manner's sake, I must grumpily lump it.

So, finally, we arrive at the alternative offered us in the heading. As I ponder it, I again remember the dinosaurs (and other such forms of life during the course of the planet's history).

Perhaps they had no time at all to adapt to changing conditions, but had to go to their dusty death only as fossils, highly interesting and informative to the curious diggers of a much later millennium.

But actually, my main concern at the moment is to follow up the warning — or threat — "adapt or die" as it applies to the human race, namely to all of us.

No doubt, an informational revolution is here with us in a big way what with computers, the Internet, and all the rest of it. We have no reason to stop it, but should find ways in which it will nourish the human spirit, not destroy it, nor become simply "technology for technology's sake." Which could indeed be the road down to our untimely human death.

Of course, it's not a physical death which we're trying to replace with a sort of earthly immortality. No, we must learn to adapt immediately and vigorously, to the present rate of change so that the human dream won't die.

In conclusion, I believe that there's enough human sanity and integrity in the world to bring us to an honourable end, whatever, in terms of God, that end may turn out to be.

Bangs and/or whimpers

Sometime in the past, someone put forth the theory that the world would end in a "big bang," and that was what led T.S. Eliot to finish one of his poems with the words "not with a bang, but a whimper" as the more likely way in which we would come to our final ignominious conclusion on earth.

Actually, I've no intention here of trying to describe such as cosmic event as the world's end, but am using Eliot's words to see whether they could apply to the way in which we choose to live, here and now, with either bangs or whimpers.

Living with bang after bang? Does it suggest to you a string of July 1 celebrations, with fireworks going off minute by minute, and rockets exploding noisily, filling the night sky with sparkles? Bangs bringing lots of excitement and fun?

Unfortunately, to me it suggests not firecrackers but guns going off, frequently at random, purposely, causing panic, pain and death.

I sometimes wonder whether the present recourse to the gun isn't, for some people, a psychological necessity. They see no other way out of a dead end. Better, they decide, to be regarded with horror than not to be be noticed at all.

Human nature can't bear to be ignored indefinitely. "Look at me!" these frustrated people cry, and bang! off goes the gun. The gun is a last desperate bid for attention, a moment at the centre of things, even on prime-time TV.

What should we be doing about it? Opening bigger and brighter casinos? Legalizing drugs? Providing longer racks of cheap bizarre clothes? But obviously these are not the solution, only a temporary escape from the problem of life's seeming meaninglessness, real or imagined.

Perhaps ours is the first time in history that the problem is being studied seriously by psychologists and sociologists, and we trust that some measure of success will attend their research.

But when it comes to a final choice between bangs and whimpers, dreadful as they may be, I choose the bangs. For me, tears should soon be wiped away or dried; weeping is only bearable and tolerable for the moment. Whimpering is only for little animals, motherless, or caught in traps.

Whimpering marks the end of human dignity.

If bangs and whimpers are both unacceptable, for what must we hope and strive? I can think of several worthy responses to make when things go wrong, but none of them comes easily. For instance, there's no stronger or nobler word in the language than fortitude; the courage to deal with life's blows, to stand up to them even though we don't feel quite able to "grin" as we bear them.

Spoiled brats and fat cats

Probably you'll not enjoy reading this article when I tell you what I have in mind. Perhaps I should even apologize in advance. You see, I'm saying that most of us in the so-called First World are both overfed as well as petulant, despite all our goodies.

Disagree, by all means, with everything in the following paragraphs, call me the worst of spoilsports, along with any other uncomplimentary names you can think of, but please be curious and broadminded enough to read and think about these things.

I know that overeating becomes almost a duty when we consider the large sums of money spent in advertising by our purveyors of food. Certainly, the scrumptiousness of the food shown and the joy of those eating it in exuberant conviviality would convince even the most committed ascetic that eating is one of the prime delights of life, and that any reproofs about gluttony be ignored or damned.

Nor am I, personally, at all averse to food, nutritious or simply attractive. No, it's the quantity consumed which I very much hold in question. How much is too much?

Most people in our highly developed industrial world do nowhere near the amount of physical work required to use up all our intake of calorie-rich foods. Most of us spend most our time sitting down in offices, cars, and/or in front of TVs. A few, it's true, do get in a few hours of jogging, golf or other such leisurely activities.

But to use up all those calories we should start digging ditches, or harvesting our corn with a machete. Instead, we ride a machine even to cut our bits of grass. Even our tots and teens seem to get most of their fun sitting down, or ambling about. No wonder, then, that they grow fat early in life, and find it difficult to lose weight later in middle-age.

In Mauritius, the overplump dodo was obviously asking for trouble and for extinction, poor bird!

Of course, there are fat people in the Third World, too. Sometimes we account for this, rather smugly, quoting their poor eating habits. Too much starch, we say, ignoring the fact that such food is the easiest to grow, and is the most filling when the stomach is empty.

Also, it's only too true that there's an elite of wealthy, privileged people in most countries, no matter how low the average income may be. I've heard this regrettable fact quoted many times over by people here in Canada who question, or

46

begrudge, sending food or money to meet the needs of an impoverished country.

Well, I'm turning now to the other unpleasant phrase used in the heading. So, how many of us deserve to be called spoiled brats? According to my dictionary, a brat is defined as "a nasty child," and so, am I, are you, behaving like nasty children? We have just about everything which we need to live reasonably healthy and happy lives, but are we satisfied and thankful?

No! Mostly we kick and scream, and throw tantrums whenever we feel the least bit short-changed. "Cut the deficit?" we cry. "But not by cutting my income?" I find this reluctance to pay up natural enough, but quite immature. Sometime in the process of growing up from querulous kids to mature adults, we should have learned to live within our means, and be prepared to handle, without too much fuss, the occasional financial cutback.

If you're thinking, at this point, how smug and censorious I'm sounding, you're quite right. So, indeed, I am! Nothing is easier than believing the best of one's own behaviour while throwing a bunch of insults at others. I myself have had such exceptionally good luck and advice handed on to me by my parents and siblings, that I can hardly take any credit for whatever wisdom I may have achieved in my old age. And so, that's that.

Those three wishes

You've probably heard, long since, about the three sisters who were granted the three wishes of their choice. It's a sad commentary on the foolishness of humanity in general, not just of that trio of benighted women. In case you've forgotten the way the story goes, here it is:

Granted the favour of the first wish, the eldest and greediest of the sisters at once wished for a big, plum pudding. Whereas the second in line, quite naturally made overhasty by her indignation, wishes that the said pudding would stick on her sister's stupid nose. Whereupon the third and last of the three felt bound in common decency to use the sole remaining wish in order to get it off again. The net result, therefore, was a rather damaged pudding in place of the magnificent might-have-been.

But now the question arises: would any of us have done any better unless we'd been given a very considerable time in which to sort out our values?

I suppose a fair number of us, if invited to "make a wish," would opt for a large sum of money, varying only from thousands to millions. I imagine, too, that quite a few would express their wish in the well known, general terms of "health and happiness," while the more practical souls among us would likely wish for something definite and immediately tangible, like the newest, most up-to-the-minute microwave oven, or a ticket (for two) to the faraway country of our choice. I fancy that only a skeptical few would turn down the opportunity of getting something for nothing by the making of a wish.

Recently I read about a rather special sort of people who are "content with little because they have so much," and I have found the description sticking in my mind like a burr. Just what is the "little," I ask myself, which can be so entirely satisfying? And what is the muchness which comes along with that sort of littleness? I suppose a lack of material things, of money and what it can buy, is the most natural way in which to interpret the "little." Well, most of us have known times, in the past, when our financial resources were much more straitened than they are today, and most of us, too, when we look back on those leaner times, will recall the wealth of a sharing, affectionate community where we were trebly rich with much faith, hope and love.

Believe me that I'm not for a moment suggesting that the poor of the world should be content with their lot of poverty. Nor that we, the more financially-blessed, should expect them to be so. Contentment is hard to come by on an empty stomach, or with an unfulfilled mind, but in the long run, it is surely the healthiest and happiest state for every wisely wishful person to choose.

There's a sense in which contentment is only a somewhat lesser word for that great word, peace. And so our three wishes might run like this: Peace for oneself, peace for one's neighbours, peace for the world.

Answering to the helm

Granted that this article's heading is somewhat enigmatic, it is, nonetheless, instructive and full of practical wisdom. And though it may have a literal application, generally speaking, it is, of course, a metaphor, and it's with the metaphorical meaning that I'm dealing here.

You might be interested in hearing about the why and whence of the topic. Well, I saw it hammered on a copper plaque which hangs on a wall in Russ Black's office. There it is shown with a ship in full sail, riding the waves, while above and below are the words: "The ship that answers not to the helm must answer to the rocks."

When I asked Russ for the story of his plaque, he told me how he'd seen a photo in Time magazine which showed the motto hung beyond the desk of a noted U.S. judge.

Russ had copied down the words for himself, and had suggested to his mother (an artist in copper-crafting) that she should incorporate them in a plaque — with the addition of a sailing vessel.

Russ himself sketched the ship for her, basing it on a photo of the famous Bluenose (which had been used in an advertisement). Ever since the 1960s, the plaque, with its message, has been an inspiration and a challenge to anyone who visits Black's office in Bracebridge.

That's the story of the plaque and its warning, briefly told. And so now follows its possible application to the lives of all us unwary sailors who must venture forth daily into unknown, often perilous seas.

What sort of helmsmen (or women) are we, casual or careful? What ship are we steering, and what rocks could cause the wreckage of our lives?

Well, you won't be surprised when I go on to say that it's each of us who must take the wheel of our metaphorical ship and steer it, carefully and conscientiously we hope, to its destination.

As for the rocks which could cause serious trouble, they are more difficult to define since they still lie hidden along future shores. But in any case they are not our chief concern — which is to grasp the wheel firmly, and keep our eyes fixed faithfully on chart and compass.

Many of us were fortunate enough to be taught a good deal about this sort of seamanship in our childhood and early youth. As the years keep rolling by, we must trust that we'll have the sense and strength, and take the time and trouble to teach ourselves to distinguish the safe and rewarding course from a disastrous one.

Fortunately for us, the steering of such a course is made much easier when we heed the accumulated wisdom of the past as it comes down to us in sayings like the one I've quoted here, even though its author and origin are unknown.

In conclusion, I think it's only fair to point out that the rocks, in themselves, are not treacherous. In fact, they are usually both beautiful and inspiring. It's our own fault if we haven't learned how to steer clear of those which could play havoc with our lives.

What is civilization?

I have before me, as I write, a clipping which has been in my file for a long time without having been brought out for further consideration and discussion. It's a quotation from a certain R. Follereau of whom I know nothing except that he seems to have made this interesting statement: "Civilization is the patient, eager, stubborn desire that there should be on earth less injustice, less pain, less unhappiness."

That word, civilization, has been around for centuries, in fact, for millennia, if we can believe the ancient writings of both East and West. Time and time again, we find that the world's wise men and prophets have stressed the necessity for justice before any people can claim its place in history as a civilized nation. Likewise, time and time again, poets everywhere have written passionately and compassionately about the pain and unhappiness suffered needlessly because of "man's inhumanity to man."

What are we to make then, of Follereau's definition? Have most of us that "patient, eager, stubborn desire" that there should be less injustice, pain, and unhappiness on earth? Or do we fuss and fume for a few days about conditions in the Middle

East, or among our native people, for instance, and then decide that any patient, eager or stubborn desire on our part is simply meaningless in the face of so many built-in ambitions and antagonisms?

I recall another quite disturbing statement made, this time, by the British writer, Sir Norman Angell (between World War One and Two, if I remember correctly) when he wrote: "Men would rather die than think." And perhaps we should add to that "They would rather kill than negotiate."

Why do our most advanced civilizations still resort so feverishly to armed conflict? Is it because our leaders cannot think deeply and clearly enough to find peaceful compromises and solutions? Is the careful study of history too exhausting and baffling a task for any but a tiny minority?

As I understand it, the word civilization, as given in my dictionary, means the very opposite of war. "Civil disobedience," for instance, is a way of demonstrating one's opposition to the government without resorting to violence. "Civility" suggests restraint, and even a measure of goodwill, certainly not belligerence in our dealings with others.

I was really astonished to find that the quotation with which I began this articled ended with the very idealistic definition that "Civilization is to love one another." At present, I find it next to impossible to imagine this planet's very diverse peoples being able to think and act in terms of love, even if we knew what love's terms would be. My most sanguine hope is that we should, to the best of our capacity, act as fairly civilized people.

The relish of a struggle

One of the worst things to face and the best to look back on is some sort of struggle. Most of us will freely admit to preferring to move from day to day easily and comfortably without having to flex our muscles unduly or screw up our courage to any sticking point. Others, we recognize, may choose to reach the North Pole on foot, dragging heavy loads over endless miles of snow and ice, but as for ourselves, we'll wait for that regular service on the Arctic Express, preferably in a nicely heated, well-lit plane. The idea that it's more fun and gives more satisfaction when you have to struggle to reach a goal, well, it seems a bit far-fetched. What can possibly be wrong in preferring to live one's life with the minimum of strain and stress?

Somehow, though, there doesn't seem to be much satisfaction in accomplishing a job too easily. Strangely enough, the easy victory is almost no victory at all — nothing to look back on with pride, with happy self-congratulation. It's only the job done, the goal reached after a session of hard work, and a bit of a struggle, which brings to the human heart a glow of satisfaction. Those intrepid adventurers, who endure great hardships in order to reach the tops of mountains or the bottoms of seas (as well as those imaginary poles at the top and bottom of the planet) — they are indeed the heroic strugglers. But, on the other hand, we mortals of the more ordinary sort can also play our part in tackling what is arduous. Although our struggles against weariness or slackness may seem trivial by comparison, they too can count for progress.

Perhaps one of the most continuous and arduous of all struggles is that of self-discovery and self-knowledge. But whereas the explorers of land, sea, and sky are often able to follow ways which have already been mapped out by their predecessors, those of us who boldly undertake the discovery of ourselves are mostly travelling into a dark, unmapped world. When some noted philosopher or psychologist, whose name I've forgotten, declared that the life which is not examined is not worth living, he was almost certainly referring to all of us ordinary people. Yet to examine one's own strengths and weaknesses, one's own psyche, if that's the appropriate word, to examine this, fairly and squarely, is a task much harder than climbing a mountain or plumbing an ocean.

Most of don't know how or where to begin the struggle to discover ourselves. We may well stare at the reflected image in a mirror and feel bewildered and appalled at the strange face which looks back at us. It gives us only the smallest of clues as to whether we are weak or strong, kind or cruel, bond or free. I added the last phrase, quoting St. Paul, because surely that's the most important discovery of all, whether we are free or are still wearing the old bonds of ignorance and prejudice.

Well, let's conclude with the happy assumption that we're not totally and hopelessly bound, but still able to struggle onward and upward with a fair degree of relish, a relish which is filled with the spice of adventurous living.

You know, and anyway

I'll begin by saying that I feel a bit mean and snobbish when I criticize other people's frequent use of "you know" and "anyway." After all, there's nothing really wrong with either of them. They certainly aren't swear words, nor are they vulgar, nor even in questionable taste. No, they're just very irritating when heard over and over again.

It seems that many people are quite unable to get through even a short speech without the interpolation of a "you know." And then there are the many others, equally irritating, who punctuate every second sentence with an "anyway."

What does it indicate, this seeming need to insert one or the other of these quite redundant, largely irrelevant expressions? I myself am probably guilty of resorting to them more often than I realize, and so I'm really checking my own psyche, too, as I begin to track down the various possible reasons for our dependence on them.

So let's look first at that oft-recurring "you know." Well, upon thinking things over and noting where the speaker usually inserts it, I've come to the conclusion that the "you know" is slipped into the stream of words to give the speaker a feeling of confidence. That's to say, if you think your listener is agreeing with what you're saying, you'll continue your speech, relieved, and assured that your opinion is being accepted, perhaps even endorsed.

None of us enjoys being alone. We all hope to have the company of our peers to give us a pleasant feeling of security. Only a really convinced (or conceited) person will readily express an unpopular point of view. And so I'm suggesting that "you know" is being inserted to give courage to the speaker. At least, that's my present, doubtlessly oversimplified explanation.

Going on now to the second of my personal bête noires, there's the frequent use of that poor little orphan-word "anyway." Actually, it rarely means a thing, and serves only to bring the narrator back again to his or her main topic. We're listening, say, to a story about what happened when our friend paid a visit to a daughter in Toronto. But en route, so to speak, there are a great number of asides so that every few minutes we have to be brought back on track with a "but, anyway."

In the course of such a narrative, I've listened to at least half-a-dozen quite unrelated asides (e.g. how my friend had trouble starting her car; how she witnessed an accident; how she had recently read in the paper about a similar accident), all of this, told in detail, before the narrator has reached her daughter's house, and with it, at last, the crisis which was the original point of the story.

Well, as I started out to prove, "anyway" would seem to be the story-teller's apology for wandering off the main track and meandering down several byways. It's only fair to note that we often find these sideroads more entertaining than the main highway of the yarn.

In conclusion, let's admit that all of us have our own stock of pet words and phrases. Personally, I've never risked counting the number of times I've used favourite, easy-to-slip-in words (like certainly, for instance), but I suspect some of you could point them out in a wink.

Crooks, cranks and crackpots

I chanced upon the three words used in this week's heading in a book I was reading recently and immediately took a fancy to them. There's the attraction of the alliteration, of course, that "cr" beginning each word.

Moreover, there's also in them a sort of wry humour. Of course, if the first word, instead of being crook had been criminal, all fun would have been lost. I certainly don't find criminals and their crimes the least bit funny. But crooks sound almost lovable and so, for that matter, do cranks and crackpots.

Then, who is a crook? Well, obviously, the crooked is neither a "straight" nor a "square", both of whom may be very respectable, but seldom amusing. Not that I actually admire a crook, but he is quite likely to add a little spice to our often-flavourless life.

I see him as a rather ingenious sort of fellow who gets what he wants without endangering anyone's life by flourishing a gun or brandishing a knife.

For instance, he might embezzle the company's funds, but he certainly wouldn't shoot the boss. (That's because, as I've implied, he is imbued with a sense of humour.)

But since space is diminishing, I'll move along now to considering the cranks. At the moment, I'm not sure whether I should include myself here among the cranks or later among the crackpots! As I see the crank, he (or she, unfortunately) suffers from some kind of obsession which makes him or her quite unpleasant to live with.

To put it more bluntly, the crankiness of the crank is not only unpleasant, but disruptive. For the crank nothing is as it should be; everything is away below par as he sees it.

For instance, if he or she is a crank about food, you can count on it that this dressing is entirely wrong for that salad; that adding even the tiniest daub of cream will completely destroy the flavour of the fruit (not to mention cholesterol!). Such crankiness seems endless, and so ends much of the pleasure of eating together around a common table.

Probably these random examples are more than enough to dispose of the cranks, so that we can move on next and last to the crackpots. Are they better or worse than the cranks; basically the same, or definitely different?

Well, in most cases, their eccentricities do make them more interesting and at times even amusing (if you don't have to live with them for long).

There's the story-telling crackpot who tells you, for the umpteenth time, how you can make ice cream from the snow growing on the trees outside; how a mouse of his learnt to trick and trap the cat.

There's nothing the crackpot can't vouch for as gospel truth. But he's neither crazy nor mentally deficient; he's honestly and quite sanely, a crackpot. Somewhere along the line of his heredity or environment, he decided that the fantastic was much to be preferred to the reasonable.

So there we have them — crooks, cranks and crackpots, all of them fringe-dwellers in our well-oriented society. But perhaps they're also the leaven which, at times, lightens the whole loaf of our usually stodgy, uninspired lumpishness.

Just one big, scrappy family

If I remember correctly, there used to be a popular card game called "Happy Families". Although I can't recall ever having played it, I presume that its aim was to gather together the cards for the various members of a family into the hands of the winning player. In this way, Mama Smith and Papa Smith would find themselves happily reunited with Jimmy Jr. and Susie-May, etc. We were an innocent and optimistic society in those earlier times.

Nowadays we accept as a fact that an unhappy estrangement is the norm, whether for our near-neighbours the Smiths and Jones or for the global family, all the men, women and children inhabiting the earth. But why, indeed, is the human family so often scrappy and so seldom happy? Is it the natural bent of humanity to be quarrelsome, forever fighting one another?

Well, If that's so, might we not contrive somehow to change such a liability into an asset? Could we not, as it were, fight a "good fight", that is, take up our swords, metaphorically speaking, in defence of truth and beauty, or in an attack on meanness of spirit? That's what William Blake undoubtedly had in mind when he wrote those lines, in the poem "Jerusalem", about not ceasing from mental fight, nor of letting one's sword sleep in one's hand. Blake was envisioning an England which would be green and pleasant, not polluted with the smoke and stench of the Satanic mills of industry.

In this late twentieth century we are still trying to sort out the good and the bad which resulted when the Industrial Revolution replaced the homebased, cottage-industries with the fuel-burning factories of Europe, and subsequently, of the whole world. So now the Third World justly feels that it has every right to get scrappy when accused of causing widespread pollution in its turn, seeing that the developed countries have been doing it consistently and carelessly for more than a couple of centuries.

Then consider our constant scrapping about boundaries, as to which lands belong to us, or how much of the oceans we can lay claim to. I've never counted up the world's total number of nations, states, or other claimants to an independent status, but it must reach several hundreds, even thousands. No longer is there much desire, it seems, for burying border hatchets in order to join into larger and friendlier communities. Of course, there are exceptions, as in present-day Europe, and perhaps in promoting free trade! But a very considerable number of us instinctively distrust any such concessions. In fact, we're ready to start a scrap about them at the earliest opportunity.

Which brings me to a reluctant conclusion: that what human

beings like and do best is to engage in a good, lively scrap! Well, so long as people's emotions and minds are outraged by some of the things going on around them, and so long as they have the energy and wit to fight the mistake and misjudgments of their fellows, just so long will our natural scrappiness have a chance to bring about, eventually, the happy global family. So, let's all of us be ardent scrappers as well as peacemakers!

FAMILY GROUP: Left to right, in the back row are Marion Bennett, Ethel (Thel) and Arthur. Gladys is standing in front. Her brothers Percy, Stanley and Harold are missing from the photo.

GLADYS BENNETT took a teaching exchange position in England in 1935-36, when this photo was taken.

FOOTLOOSE AND FANCY FREE: Gladys Bennett (left) and her sister, Thel, toured Greek ruins during a Mediterranean cruise in 1973.

CHAPTER THREE: TRAVEL TALK

The Grand Tour

There was a time, back a century or two ago, when it was fashionable for young Englishmen to make what was then known as the "Grand Tour," namely, an extended visit to such culturally advanced countries as France and Italy.

Lord Byron, for instance, spent no fewer than seven years in his wanderings from Portugal to Turkey, writing many of his romantic poems along the way.

But it's not to these former literary and cultural journeys that the heading refers. Nor does it refer to the whiz-bang, all-inclusive tours which are made today by some ambitious world travellers.

Usually such tours aim to touch down at all (and only) the high spots in their itineraries which fly from London to Paris, to Rome (or from Toronto to Hong Kong, to Bangkok).

Believe me, I don't mean that such flying visits are worthless, far better that kind than none at all! But my own idea of modern grand-touring would include at least some bits and pieces of the whole civilized world. It's not nearly enough these days to "do Europe," or to go looking merely for one's "roots," whether they're back in Tobermory or Timbuktu.

Naturally, a grand tour of the whole globe can't be done all at once, and certainly not by the average working man or woman, even in our so affluent part of it. No, it takes a good deal of both time and money, and has to be accomplished over a number of years along with a good deal, too, of thoughtful planning.

And, of course, I concede, most regretfully, that for many people such travelling is quite impossible because of inescapable commitments, and ties of many other sorts, including ill health.

But in this article I'm looking at a personal and positive side of things, and asking you, my readers, to do so, too, especially those who may be in a position to influence the younger people around them.

All too often a pattern of stickiness and stuffiness is taken for granted in a bright new part of the world like Canada. Having made the one big venturesome move from some older land and culture, whether Scotland or Poland, for instance, many Canadians have developed no feelings of curiosity, nor of commitment, to all the other countries which are yet unknown to them.

A large number of our immigrants (including those of us who came a century or so ago) do indeed find the time and money needed to return "home," whether it's to Europe, South America, or even to Asia. But as I see it, that's not really expanding either their knowledge nor their sympathies.

It's merely confirming their memories and their natural loyalties. No, what I'm aiming to promote is the kind of global awareness, appreciation and concern which should surely be the mark of the 21st century.

Perhaps we've already begun this process of widening our cultural horizons with recent conferences being held in Rio de Janeiro and Tokyo, as well as in Geneva and Ottawa. I've just recently heard that the next big conference about women's special interests is being sponsored by the Chinese, probably to be held in Beijing.

But I'm not quite finished yet! Because in this last paragraph I'd like to make sure that all our stay-at-homes realize they, too, can make the grand tour of the world, savouring all its cultures, sharing all its problems and achievements by simply keeping wide-open their hearts and minds.

How dull it is to pause

I'm calling on the poet Tennyson to provide me with a heading and a theme. The words I've quoted above come from the poem "Ulysses," familiar to most of us, I think.

In it, the Greek hero-adventurer, Ulysses, declares in round terms that he's not at all content to stay quietly at home in Itheca (matched, as he says, with an aged wife, poor fellow). So he announces forthwith that he's going off on another voyage, aiming this time "to sail beyond the sunset." Moreover, he's quite ready, it seems, to risk being drowned in the ocean which lies beyond the Gates of Hercules — that's to say, when he passed Gibraltar at the western end of the Mediterranean Sea.

Although I don't aspire to being nearly so daring as Ulysses, I do heartily agree with him that staying at home can be very boring. Thus it is that after only a few weeks of day-to-day living in a small town like Bracebridge (nice as it certainly is), I become increasingly restive. "How dull it is to pause," I mutter to myself, "to make an end!" And so I begin to dream of all those faraway places which I've not yet seen. I conjure up in imagination all their possible charms and thrills, so far unsavoured. Some of us, like old Ulysses, are inveterate seekers after the exotic and exciting. Even though we concede that the flood may wash us down somewhere, we're determined to enjoy all we can of the novelty, excitement, and beauty which the planet has to offer. Ulysses went mainly by boat, while I go footloose by bus, train, ship, or plane. Who cares so long as it goes!

Now, obviously there are a large number of very worthy people who live out their lives within a relatively limited sphere of action. In Ulysses' case it was his son Telemachus who was quite happy to remain at home and govern Itheca. And presumably that's the way many other stay-at-homes see things. But, on the other hand, if it's a lack of money which keeps them from travelling or feeling of obligation to others, I'm genuinely sorry because of all that's being missed.

Fancy never having seen the rosy glow of a sunrise on the Alps or the Himalayas! Never to have gazed down in wonder on a long white beach in Hawaii or Australia! Never to have mingled with a crowd of smiling Chinese along a street in Beijing, or watched a gaggle of excited black youngsters come careening, pell-mell down an African hillside!

Impressions of South Africa

For the first-time visitor to South Africa its most impressive feature is likely to be its spectacular coast. However, it's difficult to give definite locations and names because there seem to be so many of them! But this most southerly region, here in Cape Province, must surely be recognized as quite exceptional. In the brilliant sunshine, the Indian Ocean along with the Atlantic are just as startlingly blue, and multi-hued, as the Mediterranean.

And added to the drama of mighty cliffs and crashing surf, there is the unexpected beauty of the many wildflowers. The proteas, South Africa's national flower, grow everywhere profusely — along the roads, in the vast fields, as well as cultivated extensively in the parks and gardens. Even more eye-catching than the proteas are the great stretches of the pinkish-purple wild geraniums, besides all manner of yellow flowering bushes! Then, again, there are the endless clumps of everlasting flowers — now being dyed in various bright colours for dried-flower arrangements.

Cape Town, situated down on the southerly tip of the province, is unquestionably one of the most scenically impressive cities in the world. Besides having Table Mountain as a magnificent backdrop, there are the stately Twelve Apostles nearby, and a sharply pointed peak called the Sentinel at the entrance to Hout Harbour. And mentioning Hout brings to mind another highlight in our sightseeing, namely a boat ride through the bright blue sea to visit a colony of seals.

Never had I imagined that so many seals, large and small, mature and young ones, could find space to breed and feed in such numbers as we saw them crowded on those small, rocky islands. Lying closely side by side, slipping in and out of the surf all around them, their skins shining black, streaming with water, they made a picture almost beyond belief. Sad to say, we learned that these seals, and other similar colonies along the coast, have created a real problem since they are eating far too many of the fish which the coastal fishermen depend on for their livelihood. So while some of us are thrilled by their numbers and activity, others are dismayed and even angered by the threat which they pose.

There's one Englishman, namely Cecil Rhodes, who was quite important in the development of South Africa, especially in Cape Province. He became, of course, a very wealthy man with a big interest in the Kimberley diamond mines, but it seems that he was very generous with his money. He bequeathed vast and valuable properties to the South African government, as well as endowing many schools and colleges. However, his dream of establishing British rule in Africa, from "Cape to Cairo," was never realized, and so, in this respect, Rhodes died a deeply disappointed man. He had emigrated from England at the age of only 17, and became a passionate lover of his adopted country.

As I write this article, here in Cape Town, we still have another two days of sight-seeing. This afternoon we fly to the neighbouring country of Zimbabwe, there to visit the famous Victoria Falls. But before leaving Cape Town and South Africa, I really must attempt a description of the beautiful view I get from my seventh storey window.

During the bright day it is a dazzling blue and white picture, with the intense, indigo-blue of the ocean and the azure of the sky combining with the startling white of the buildings as they climb, rank above rank, up Table Mountain, up to Lion's Head. Then, later, about seven o'clock, as the sun is dropping into the ocean, everything is suffused with lovely tints of yellow and orange, rose and mauve, and the mountain is covered with twinkling lights. I might even say that this one view has been worth the trip to South Africa!

What's special about Ecuador?

So, what's special about this small South American country? Well, at once comes the response, "Why, the Galapagos, of course!" Yes, a great many people seem to have read or heard about this little archipelago lying some 600 miles off the coast of Equador with its strange creatures such as the giant tortoises and booby birds.

But, I must add, in protest, that the Ecuadorean mainland has at least one other noted specialty, and that's Quito's quite outstanding treasure of Spanish-American colonial architecture. These buildings in Quito have been duly and fully recognized as a "World Heritage" by the United Nations Organization. And, personally, I admit to being far more fascinated by these magnificent, gilded churches than by the rather weird fauna (and flora) of the Galapagos. Nonetheless, I'm not at all surprised that so many tourists are so irresistibly attracted to these island cruises.

A cruising ship is a truly delightful way of moving to and fro among the islands, being (as far as my one experience goes) very well-designed, equipped, and serviced. Our "Santa Cruz" accommodated about 70 passengers along with the appropriate staff and crew — just about the right size for a few days of pleasant companionship. Certainly the atmosphere on our ship was one of shared interest and enthusiasm.

Since the Santa Cruz was too big to tie up at most of the islands visited, we always had the excitement of going down (and returning up again) a flight of steps placed securely to the ship's side, and of boarding a raft-like sort of boat called a panga. I particularly enjoyed our "wet" landings when we were assisted, or hoisted, over the raft's side, and then waded through the warm surf up to the sandy beach, usually a splendid, tawny-red colour.

Although some of the Galapagos specials are easily seen without the aid of binoculars, I, for one, would have welcomed the loan of a strong pair in order to locate and identify the many species of birds, as well as some of the smaller lizards and iguanas. But the larger ones, like the cormorants, pelicans, frigate birds, and not-to-be forgotten flamingos, are there to delight the ordinary naked eye, and, and course, the sea-lions and their cute, bug-eyed babies are a constant cause for joy. Cutest of all, for me, were the Sally Lightfoot crabs skittering about the rocks in a magic world of colour.

But before running out of space, I must again mention the quite fabulous grandeur and charm of Quito's churches and monasteries. Moreover, there's all that magnificent scenery as you travel down to the lovely towns of Baños and Cuenco. Then, too, there's the colourful kaleidoscope of markets and crafts; and always the Ecuadoreans themselves, a beautiful and vital people, despite much lingering poverty.

Trip to Bulgaria was enjoyable

It's a fact that people couldn't look more startled if I'd told them I'd been to the moon. Bulgaria! You must be crazy! That's the normal response. To Florida, of course. To California, that's nice. To Hawaii, how exciting. But to Bulgaria?

Well, I've explained to a dozen or so people that the attraction to Sophia (Bulgaria's capital) was a week of special music and some New Year's festivities as arranged by the Congress Tours. Moreover, the trip was relatively inexpensive, and the accommodation at a Sheraton Hotel was excellent. The fact that it ventured into Eastern Europe wasn't all that off-putting to anyone who knows the difference between Zagraeb and Sophia, Croatia and Bulgaria. And you can see from this article that I'm back safe and sound, and quite pleased with my New Year's jaunt.

There was glorious choral music in the vast Nevski Cathedral which was all lit up and wired up for the occasion. Equally thrilling was a symphony concert featuring Japanese music. The orchestra, a really large one, was Sophia's own, but the conductor and soloists were Japanese. The main item on the program, called "Hiroshima," had words written by an English poet. And the hall's acoustics were superb.

The New Year's Eve party was a gala affair. It had a sumptuous buffet lunch, and lots of lively music, favours, and balloons.

When midnight struck, the whole hotel staff, including the cooks and bottlewashers, joined in the dancing and hoopla.

Probably Bulgaria is also having its troubles as it moves away from a communist economy, but apparently it's managing to do so without panic or violence. The streets, as we saw them, were busy with trams, taxis, cars and pedestrians, while the stores were busy with customers (and were still decorated with silvery reindeer and lots of tinsel). Naturally, things are not so plush as here in Canada — they never have been — but so far as the casual visitor can see, the people are quite adequately fed and clothed (many of the children's coats are as brightly coloured as those seen here).

And in winter, much of the Bulgarian countryside is outstandingly beautiful with its two snow-peaked mountain ranges. Driving along highways and byways to reach the Rila Monastery, and the famous old town of Plovdiv, we were constantly exclaiming at the beauty of the landscape. Into the bargain, we vicariously enjoyed the excitement of the many skiers, bright spots of colour on the snowy slopes.

The weather? It was much the same as here in Ontario, giving us a couple of days with damp cold winds, then deciding to relent and become sunny and comparatively balmy. Parts of Bulgaria are so sheltered by its mountains that its vineyards and orchards are famous in Europe. Of course, it has a string of summer resorts along the western shore of the Black Sea, but we saw nothing of them in January! Perhaps I'll return at a later, warmer date, and hear again those incredulous cries of "Not Bulgaria!"

From Cyprus with love

You might be surprised at the number of times I've talked about Muskoka during the week since I left home. Everyone on this tour is interested (they come all the way from Halifax to Vancouver) and many of them speak of Muskoka in very appreciative terms. But, of course, at present, we're all more interested in Cyprus, and I imagine that's what you're expecting to hear about in this article. Here goes!

Actually, I've been here in Limassol for less than a week, since reaching it from Toronto takes time even by air, especially when a stop, overnight, is made in London en route. Our tour group is now well established in one of the many fine hotels along this southern coast, enjoying the bright sunshine and blue sea.

Spread out between us and the Mediterranean are the hotel gardens with their outdoor swimming pools, including a small stream with a series of tiny waterfalls! I've already wandered about the gardens taking pictures, and found there so many different sorts of flowers to photograph that I had to call a halt in case I used up all my film.

So far, any touring of the island has been limited to yesterday's coach trip to nearby Limassol and other local attractions. In the city itself, it was mainly for shopping in the older streets, now set apart for pedestrians. I wandered briefly up and down admiring, especially, the superb crochet; I priced a blouse at $30 Canadian. As in many resorts, the shops are full of knick-knacks, probably imported, but with many of them also being picturesque, I took pictures!

More interesting was the countryside where we passed

through extensive groves of orange trees, laden with great balls of fruit, rows upon rows; along with them were grapefruit and lemons, a citrus paradise. And now the avocado is being introduced on a large scale. We were told that a great deal of this fertile land was formerly a swamp, infested by a malarial-type of mosquito.

I was particularly impressed by the long stretches of tall, slender cypresses growing along both sides of the road. Our guide explained that they had been planted there to cut down the force of the wind blowing in from the sea. I should mention here, too, the rows of plastic greenhouses for the growing of strawberries. We were lucky enough to make a pause beside them to buy packages of the juicy, ripe fruit.

We reached the highlights of yesterday's tour with visits to two historic sites. The first of these was a three storey, stone castle, set four-square above the sea. It dates back to the Middle Ages when the Crusaders were travelling to and from the Holy Land. The most familiar of them, for us, was King Richard of England, known as the Lion-hearted. And, by the way, the same Richard was married here in Cyprus to his Queen Berengaria.

The second of the notable places seen yesterday was the site of ancient Kutrium. There, recent excavations have uncovered a splendid Roman amphitheatre set into the hillside, as well a many fine, mosaic tile floors in its former villas. Since Kutrium was located high up on a hilltop, the view from it, looking down on the coast and the sea, is especially beautiful.

The terrain at Kutrium is still rough with rocks, large and small, fixed and shifting, and so walking can be hazardous, but with helpful hands stretched out to steady me over the worst of them, I managed not too badly. I can only hope that the wobble in my knees wasn't transmitted disastrously to the camera in my hands.

For the present, I think that's enough about Cyprus. Perhaps I should add that there's a general disarray of unfinished buildings along this coast near Limassol. Everywhere are piles of dirt and stones, and frequently the sea front and its promenade is somewhat unkempt. It seems that the older, well-developed resorts are now in the areas taken over by the Turkish-Cypriots. However, at the pace they're working here, it won't be long before everything will be set right.

There are several more day trips to be made on this tour — for instance, to Nicosia, the capital, and to the lofty Troodos Mountains. More of them when I get back!

Walking with Thel in Scotland

Quite by chance the other day I came upon an old diary of mine written way back in the 1930s when Thel and I spent a summer holiday in England and Scotland (and Ireland, too), mostly hiking. I'm using a few pages of it for this article since it comes apropos of my comment last week that Thel and I had enjoyed many a walk together. This particular trek (being in Scotland) included a good deal of rain! We were making our way in the neighbourhood of Morar and Mallaig, when the following adventures befell us. Hereon I quote.

"We had about six miles that morning before we reached shelter at Skyeview (of course, Skye was totally blotted out!)

Since most of the walk was done in a driving rain, we presented a thoroughly bedraggled appearance when Mrs. Cameron took us in. We were very lucky in coming upon Skyeview; we had a cozy room, appetizing meals, friendly fellow-sufferers, and a chance to dry out our sodden garments. Thel's skirt had got soaked around the hem, and since we had brought her no change along that line, she had to retire under the comforter until the kitchen stove had done its job. My shorts were properly high and dry under my mac, and so I simply had to rub myself down and put on fresh shoes and stockings.

"Neither of us seemed to suffer from our little shower-bath, and although we felt rather miserable while plodding through the rain, in retrospect it's all part of the fun. It gives you such a feeling of independence to discover that you can tramp along in foul weather as well as in fair!

"The next morning seemed a bit brighter and so we set out again, and enjoyed about five miles of woodland before another steady drizzle drove us to the nearby railway to await the mid-day train. We used it for the few remaining miles to Lochaillart, having it specially stopped for our benefit. We felt like royalty stepping out, though somehow we had taken our ride in the baggage van. We had made up our minds to rise to the level of a hotel bill in Lochaillart — it being such a tiny place, we couldn't expect much choice. As it chanced, we found ourselves comfortably established for the next two nights in the station-master's spare room.

"Our window looked out on a tiny burn which scampered under a stone bridge. These arched bridges of grey or brown stone are lovely things. Some are just little humps of one span, looking like a rockery with all their baby ferns and flowers growing in the crevices. Beyond our burn rose the mountains, ridge beyond ridge, but we never saw the complete skyline; always some part of it was veiled in mist. Actually, I'm glad that those peaks were never wholly exposed; as it was, they symbolized the beauty which 'passes knowledge.'

"Since the next morning promised to be fairly clear, we strode off, up hill and down dale. The first incident of note that day was the skirting of Loch Dubh, another 'dark pearl' of the Highlands. We tried persistently to locate the spot from which we could awaken the echo about which Margaret Boyd (an English friend) had told us. The I found it at last, and with what delight we listened for the replies to our calls! There's an unearthly beauty in an echo; Tennyson expressed it rightly when he said that it came from Elfland.

"Not far from Loch Dubh we began a rough-and-tumble three miles to a luncheon spot high up among rocks and bog. It sounds a dismal sort of goal, but oh, the joy of plunging across open hillsides with clean sod underfoot, clean air all around you, and the sea stretching out towards Rumm, Eigg, and Skye!"

So, what about Iceland?

As usual, my thoughts are much too numerous to put down in just a few paragraphs, and so any attempt here to sum up my impression of Iceland is sure to fall far short of a fair coverage. And you'll be looking in vain for any references to Greenland which was also included in this recent tour because that would certainly sink the ship of my column.

You won't be at all surprised, I'm sure, when I list neatness and cleanliness as the first of one's impressions of Iceland. Many of you have visited the Scandinavian countries and so at once will recognize the transference of their clean culture to Iceland. Cities and countrysides are both equally tidy in appearance; fresh and refreshing to the eyes. Iceland has its share of economic woes (resulting mainly from the cod fisheries crisis in the North Atlantic), but there is, at present, anyway, no sign of poverty nor of economic stress.

The second most interesting impression I got in and of Iceland, was the importance of its present unlimited supply of hot water coming from geothermal heat. For the ordinary visitor this is clearly visible in plumes of steam rising from holes, fissures, and pools in the ground everywhere. One learns only gradually how this boon of free hot water has enabled Icelanders to have domestic and industrial heating at an amazingly low cost. The guides, of course, know all about this earthborn (heaven-sent?) blessing, and so visitors quickly learn to appreciate it, too. There's even talk nowadays of exporting hot water to Europe through a transatlantic pipeline!

I pass next to some comments upon Iceland's varied scenery. Somehow I had formed a personal preconception of endless tundra, surrounded, of course, by the ocean. Well, it's true that there are wide stretches of flat land covered with lumpy, bumpy lava boulders, some of them dating back to long-past millennia. Nevertheless, the chief impression for me was the wealth of greenery. No wonder the Vikings, and later the Danes, were drawn to this island in the far north if they came upon it during its springtime verdure! And succeeding generations of enterprising and energetic Icelandic farmers have largely cleared the land of its lava waste, and created verdant pastures, rich and beautiful. Moreover, there's a real concern in

Iceland today to extend the greenness in order to beat the ever-present threat of erosion. Consequently, the planting of trees goes on steadily (in their summer holidays, school students do a great deal of it as government employees). Private house-holders, too, in Reykjavik especially, are surrounding their homes with trees and bushes of all kinds.

But I should move on to other impressions. I've already men-tioned the charm of Iceland's greenness, but to that must be added the blue, purple and red of mountains, and the quite spectacular cliffs. Up in the mountains one finds glaciers and ski resorts, and down on the coasts the white surf, breaking on black rocks and beaches. Volcanic eruptions have created in Iceland a magical sort of scenery which seems to compensate, to a large degree, for the havoc they are bound to cause. It's rather surprising that most Icelanders don't seem to pay much attention to the dangers posed by the volcanoes but rather enjoy the excitement they promise or threaten.

Finally, I'm not sure whether it rates as a major impression, but I was certainly struck by the fair-skinned homogeneity of the Icelandic people. So far, the recent mass migrations taking place throughout the more southerly parts of the world have hardly touched Iceland. Probably most people seek easier cli-mates and a more industrialized society, and so have not been attracted to the rim of the Arctic Circle. Consequently, the vis-itor finds there a non-multicultural population, living quietly among themselves, much as their foreparents did for centuries.

Well, this article has gone on much longer than usual, and I still have plenty more to say about Iceland, and there's Greenland yet to come! But all that will have to wait for a later date. Meanwhile, I hope you've enjoyed these off-the-cuff impressions. (My slides are quite good, I'm pleased to say!)

Impressions of Newfoundland

As the plane descended into St. John's airport at Torbay, I was amazed to see that we were gliding over a green, green world. Somehow my memories from a long-ago former visit were of mainly grey rocks, and ragged trees, interspersed with sheets of steel-grey water. But this time the green below rivalled the Emerald Isle itself.

This first lush impression was confirmed as we drove into St. John's, passing along avenues lined with green trees and shrubbery where every house seemed to be fronted by a well-groomed lawn. Moreover, I was really surprised to see all around evidences of a relatively high standard of living. Is this, I asked myself, our hard-hit impoverished tenth province? This is one of the neatest and nicest cities I have ever seen!

Well, of course, neatness and cleanliness come not so much with wealth, but as the result of a caring tradition. It would seem that once the Newfoundlanders have even a small amount of money behind them, they have the will to spruce things up to the maximum. Very few houses are shabby with peeling paint disfiguring them. Now they are well-kept, smooth and charming in a wide variety of pastel tints, or strong, warm colours. It's a constant delight to see them climbing up hillsides, or edging the ponds or ocean shores.

Even right around here in the Avalon Peninsula, there is plenty of variety in the scenery. One moves quickly from the trim city streets to the rugged shores, from tidy lawns and cultivated flowers to untidy forests, rock-strewn fields, and shallow (but picturesque) ponds. And the wildflowers are everywhere: daisies, buttercups, lupins, roses, even Newfoundland's floral emblem, the pitcher plant.

Nor are historical sights missing. There are relics of the wars between England and France, battlements and cannon. And from those early years, we move on to the laying of the transatlantic cable, and the first wireless which occurred, respectively, in the 19th and 20th centuries.

And finally, during this Horizon Tour, a visit to the hillside monument which marks the spot where Churchill and Roosevelt met, off-shore, in 1941, to join their forces to win World War Two and lay plans for a safer, saner world. Out of that meeting came the Atlantic Charter and the first steps towards the founding of the U.N.O.

During the tour I've been taking pictures as usual, lucky to be blessed with sunny weather from day to day, the whole week through. Perhaps I should make a partial exception of the morning we put out to sea to make a cold, blustery voyage to Bird Island. However, any discomfort we felt was more than compensated for by the thousands of gulls (of many species) plus a whole circus of adorable, clowning puffins.

What else should be included in these preliminary general impressions and comments? Well, certainly no one visits Newfoundland without experiencing the friendliness of its people. They almost overwhelm you at times with their kindliness. Doubtless, they are very proud of their island homeland, its past, present and future, but they are far too generous and polite to make any invidious remarks about the rest of Canada!

Off to China

This is the fifth time in the past 30 years that I've flown across Canada and over the Pacific to the People's Republic of China. So what's the attraction there? Because I've sometimes asked myself that same question, I'm now trying to answer it.

No doubt curiosity has been one continuing motive, always wanting to find out what's really happening over there. Fortunately, in my travels I've never been put off by tales about communism or by any other such political differences.

My interest is based mainly on a country's history, with an emphasis on its sociology. China is especially interesting since it keeps changing course and developing, always doing so in its own lively, cheerful fashion. At least, in the past 30 years I've always found the Chinese people full of smiling vivacity.

China has had an amazing history, going back for abut 5,000 years, with wonders now to be seen in its museums, tombs, temples and palaces. It's very conscious of its past glories and its inherited arts, and is eager to share them with any westerners who show genuine interest in them.

Unfortunately, most tourists can only wander around and gawk a bit, unable to appreciate the ancient bronzes, fine chinaware, and exquisite paintings. But a great deal of this artistry lives on among the quite ordinary Chinese people, even though it is being sorely tempted nowadays to drop down to the level of cheap souvenirs hawked along the streets and on parking lots.

Another good reason for returning to China is its superb scenery. More and more cruises are being offered along rivers like the Yangtze, famous for its spectacular gorges, and the River Li, bordered by picturesque villages and fantastic mountain peaks. And not to be ignored are the stretches of green and shining rice fields.

If you travel north into Inner Mongolia, there are wide, windswept plains where horses still race freely with manes flying.

What else? Of course, there are the well-known greats like the Great Wall, winding up and down over the hills as it has done for more than 2,000 years, a monument to dynastic and patriotic pride.

And close at hand, in Beijing, the Imperial City is full of architectural and ornamental delights in marble, bronze and richly painted red and gold. Surely, no one would willingly miss seeing the beautiful Temple of Heaven. Or the Marble Boat, solidly stuck as a handsome pavilion in the waters of West lake, a reminder of the stupid selfishness of the final, inglorious Manchu dynasty.

But after noting all these good reasons for visiting and revisiting China, it really comes down to the people themselves, their cheerfulness, their industry, their optimism. I shall be very much surprised if I find anyone "down in the dumps," talking of some possible "doom and gloom."

Their present bustling entry into world-wide affairs may lead the Chinese into a kind of brashness and, being human, even into occasional skulduggery, but I have complete faith in their basic decency and good sense.

Both Confucius and Mao have given them plenty of sound advice which they're unlikely to forget in a hurry. Moreover, I shall also be very much surprised if anyone treats me curtly, rather than courteously, especially since I'm grey-haired and come from the same country as Dr. Norman Bethune!

A Gaspésian holiday

If you're puzzled by the keyword in this article's heading, you could consult a map of Canada and there locate the Gaspé Peninsula jutting out into the Atlantic. It's a prominent feature of the eastern coast and a very popular holiday resort, especially for the Quebec people.

My friend Dorothy and I reached it by air and then hired a car. That enabled us to drive along the coast, enjoying en route the parks and villages as well as the scenery.

It seems that there's still a fair amount of commercial fishing, and so I had the chance to photograph the boats and other colourful bits and pieces of gear, like the big traps used now for catching crabs and lobsters.

Of course, the Gaspésians also sell souvenirs, and so shops and studios occur frequently in the villages and along the roadsides. Most of our own purchases were made in Percé, the centre of the resort area.

It's an exceptionally charming town, boasting many attractions in addition to its famous pierced rock and the bird colony on nearby Bonaventure Island. Although some of the Percé shops are full of the usual "junk," many of them do specialize in various crafts.

I particularly liked the articles made from polished stones, like the local agate, and I bought a small slab that shows a pattern of darkish brown rings on a creamy background.

My friend and I were very fortunate with our accommodations, in both Gaspé town and in Percé. In the former, the Adams Motel is located right at the centre of things (such as an excellent, though small, museum).

Moreover, from it, a road leads directly to the beautiful Forillon Park, giving lots of opportunities en route to visit a dozen or so delightful capes and coves. If one is still young and energetic, there are also hiking trails leading to other attractions, like La Chute, a waterfall.

Of course, there are also well-maintained picnic grounds.

In Percé we were even luckier. There we stayed in a smallish motel, La Bellevue, right beside the ocean. Moreover, along the front was a boardwalk where we could stroll at our ease, admiring the coastal scenery, including an excellent view of the Rock, and enjoying the fresh, salty breezes.

Into the bargain, we were within easy walking distance of La Pigalle, a restaurant where both the food and the service were most satisfactory.

As for the people of Quebec, the Quebécois, we found them invariably friendly to us Ontarians; and even when we tried out our feeble French, they accepted our efforts as admirable, not absurd (as, most often, they probably were!).

Impressions of Malawi

Probably some of you are already aware that I've recently returned from visiting parts of Southern Africa, namely, the countries of Zimbabwe, Zambia and Malawi.

Before too long I hope to be showing the slides taken in all three of them, but in this article I'm referring only to Malawi. That's not because it's necessarily the most interesting, but simply that I find it easier to stick to just one country and my impressions of it, rather than skip around commenting on all three.

So what about Malawi? Well, in the first place, like many other countries in Africa, it has a colonial past, having been for several decades part of the British Empire and Commonwealth, governed from Westminster in London, England, until it attained independence in the 1960s.

Consequently, modern Malawi strikes the Western visitor as still being partly English. That's to say, the English language is widely spoken, and the food served in the hotels is largely familiar.

But having noted these familiarities, one immediately recalls the many differences, the general strangeness of things. For, of course, the Malawian people everywhere are black.

Only in such places as airports and hotels can one count on seeing a white face or, for that matter, a brown or Oriental one. But after a while this becomes part of the attraction of the scene, specially since the blacks are such a good-natured people.

When individuals of the various races meet in Malawi, they are most often talking business, seeking to establish trade links, or making some sort of deal. So you see them getting together in the hotel lounges or restaurants, bringing out their books and papers in mutual serious consultation.

Naturally enough, I gravitated to the white people whenever I got an opportunity to do so, since it was much easier for me to converse with them, and ask them questions. In most cases they seemed quite pleased to talk to me, describing their line of business, or their temporary job, paid or voluntary.

In the course of my week in Malawi I met a team of two Swiss and Danish engineers who were concerned with some aspects of transportation and communication.

Then there was an American doctor and an English nurse, both of whom were involved in health services, he in checking clinics scattered throughout the country, and she as head nurse in a town hospital.

I think the most interesting contact I chanced to make was with an English marine biologist (at least, that's my own amateurish way of describing him). He was there to develop more extensive and profitable ways of fishing in Lake Malawi.

In the past, the catch has been pretty well confined to offshore fishing, done in small boats launched nightly. This "expatriate" scientist was there to promote and encourage deeper, mid-lake fishing, using bigger boats, and getting a larger and more diversified catch.

This, of course, brings with it the need for local boat-building of a larger, more sophisticated kind, and the inevitable, essential financing!

Do you see where all this is leading us? It's the old story of sharing the world's know-how, not condescendingly but happily. This Britisher in Malawi is an excellent example of that sort of helpful, enthusiastic sharing.

He had already done stints of similar work in places as far apart as Turkey and Nicaragua! How refreshing and reassuring it is to find so much positive good out there as I found it among these expatriate scientists and the people of Malawi!

The globe and I

Some of you may recall that I recently wrote an article entitled "About the chickadees and me," inspired by what goes on in my back yard. Well, this week's topic is considerably broader in that it takes us around the globe, with its manifold sights and peoples.

Perhaps I've previously mentioned that I bought for myself a small globe, neatly made and turning gently on its axis? I like to set it in motion while I think about the people who inhabit its many, various countries.

Some of them I've visited, usually returning for a second or third look. Always there is the unknown, or only partly known, to keep me going back.

If I listed the countries I've visited it would be merely a string of names, about 70 or 80 of them, causing you to raise an eyebrow perhaps. But their number is of secondary importance; the main thing is their impact on me, the lessons I've learnt, the pleasures felt.

Possibly natural beauty is easiest to appreciate: blue seas, snow-capped mountains, gloriously coloured flowers, and much besides.

Once seen, they are never completely forgotten.

But equally wonderful and memorable, it seems to me, are our human achievements, some dating from the distant past, others richly present.

For us Westerners the Parthenon symbolizes all we owe to Greece, and later to Rome, in architecture, philosophy, literature, science, law, and even politics — the list is endless.

But in Iran, once the centre of the vast Persian Empire, I discovered the incredible beauty and majesty of Persepolis, that magnificent complex of triumphal gates (to Darius to Xerxes), and ceremonial halls reached by elegant flights of steps, all delicately carved, all dug out of the sand to astonish and delight our eyes.

I am reminded of all this, and much more, as I twirl my globe around and see the continents in quick succession, and in-between them the wide and wonderful blue of the oceans.

But if we are a caring people we have to stop this fascinating and easy motion, and come down to earth to learn what life is like for the rest of the human family, born and bred to share its joys, sorrows and mysteries.

As Christmas comes, I see, in retrospect, the smiling and troubled faces — black, brown, pink, and white; the sparkling eyes, the anxious eyes; hands skilful and hands trembling with age or illness.

In imagination, I see many lights set burning as people express their faith, in the flickering of candles, or emblazon it in strings of bulbs, electrically brilliant.

Most of us realize, many with a feeling of shame, how little we are doing to bring the smiles, sparkling eyes, steady hands, and all the rest that means health and happiness, to wherever they are still not part of life on the globe.

In this season of goodwill to all, the extra prayer, the extra loonie might make a mite of difference, somehow, somewhere.

CHAPTER FOUR:
THIS 'N' THAT

Sharing the wealth

I'm not sure who first coined the slogan which heads this week's article, perhaps some economist with leanings to the left. Certainly there are many well-to-do people who are distressed when they see the rich becoming "too rich and the poor too poor". That's to say when the imbalance is so marked that everyone's bound to see it.

However, I'm treating the topic in a slightly different way from just the uneven distribution of material goods. I'm thinking more of other sorts of wealth which it would be good to share more generously. For instance, education and health care. It's true that something has already been done along those lines through the efforts of churches and of organizations like Oxfam and CUSO, but that's only a beginning. We, who are comparatively well-off here in Canada, with our many schools and hospitals could easily become quite insensitive to the illiteracy and ill-health which spoil life for many of our fellow-citizens in today's world.

Sometimes we forget, too, the fact that wealth includes such intangibles as art and other forms of culture. It's always difficult for people to break the bonds of their own inherited wealth, and so most of us here cling to the European ways of thinking and feeling and only very reluctantly become aware of other cultures, like those of Africa and Asia. We'd much prefer all the other continents and their peoples to accept our forms of culture rather than learn how to blend and harmonize theirs with ours. Appreciating and sharing in the insights and achievements of other lands is one of the world's greatest needs as we move into the twenty-first century.

That's why I always rejoice when people tell me about their ventures across seas and skies in order to savour the sometimes alien cultures of Continental Europe, of Africa or Asia, for instance. Having once strolled along the boulevards of Paris or Moscow; explored the marketplaces of Marrakesh or Abidjan; or shared the crowded streets of Beijing or New Delhi, they are then much better equipped to recognize the wonderful exciting diversity of the planet, and more ready to share its cultural wealth.

However, perhaps the most desirable way of sharing the world's wealth is in fair exchange, giving and receiving with equal benefit and pleasure. The human family, though scattered far and wide by miles of land and water, can come close together when its members exchange greetings in the language of goodwill and mutual respect.

But besides material goods and cultural achievements, surely we need to share the wealth of happiness? Surely sadness should be only a passing phase in people's lives? With so much beauty and variety all around us everywhere surely it isn't beyond our ken to imagine a world full of laughter? Every time a child's face lights up, a woman smiles, or a man chuckles, there has been a sharing of affection, of some passing pleasantry.

To "share the wealth" of a beautiful, garden-like planet with a loving, family-like community of peoples, that's the best sort of sharing I can envisage in a too-often troubled and unhappy world.

Might the robin replace the beaver?

Recently I've been thinking, seriously, of suggesting to the powers-that-be in Ottawa that we change our national emblem from the beaver to the robin.

Now I ask you, isn't there something distinctively Canadian about the robin as we observe him (or her) hopping around our gardens? There's his (or her) apparently casual but undoubtedly purposeful pursuit of life's business.

For instance, home building, shopping around for food, but pausing occasionally for a breather and a cheerful, gossipy sort of comment upon life in general and his neighbours in particular, delivered without making any sort of claim to its being an operatic aria, but just a tuneful, uninhibited declaration of goodwill, (with a modest touch of self-satisfaction).

Doesn't it all sound typically Canadian?! And much more appropriate for our emblem than that sober-sided hard-working, over industrious rodent (?) the beaver.

Not that I have anything specific against the beaver, though a family of them just about cleaned out a hillside that edges the

Falkenburg swamp. It's simply that the beaver, admirable as he is, is just a bit stodgy as he ploughs through the water, cuts and hauls timber, even when he gives that resounding whack with his tail.

It seems to me that his image as an industrious worker no longer applies, for better or for worse, to the average Canadian. No doubt our forebears did clear the land with much the same commitment and perseverance as the beavers (and with a similar lack of judgement and foresight?), but nowadays things have slowed down and eased up, and most of us frequently take time off to mosey around, casually, in our pleasantly green gardens.

Now I certainly wouldn't want you to come to the conclusion that I'm in favour of a dilettante style of living, let alone of laziness.

No, the robin, it seems to me, does a very good job of carrying on in a changing world, cheerfully providing for himself and his family while at the same time contributing generously to the community with his debonair demeanor and his lilting music. Nothing world-shaking, it's true, but, on the whole, rather heart warming, and that's not such a bad role for Canada to play in our troubled, competitive, often distressful world.

Let's talk about the weather

Talking about the weather has always, it seems, been the readiest means of escape from an uncomfortable silence.

You meet someone on the street to whom you can't put a name, can't fit into a known background, and so you say brightly, "Isn't this a lovely day!" Or maybe you have to think up, on the spur of the moment, something different like, "My, isn't that a nasty wind?"

Or perhaps you find yourself seated next to someone in a bus, or at a tea table, with whom you have little or nothing in common. Probably you hesitate to introduce the subject of her family because you've heard rumors of a break-up or some other trouble. So again you take refuge in talking about the "storm that surprised us all last night" and go on from that to becoming quite verbose about the changeableness of the weather for several years past!

It's the changeableness of our so-called temperate climate which gives us so much scope for frequent and lengthy talk about it. No sooner have we good cause to complain loud and long about the cold winds, than the weather turns quite unseasonably warm and stuffy. One day we volubly lament the fact that the snow keeps falling, and then the next complain with lots of details, how the rain is flooding our basement again. We get ourselves all ready to celebrate a winter carnival with piles of crisp, firm snow and then feel properly frustrated when the weekend brings only slush.

Unfortunately, it's not much different when we leave home to travel abroad. At the airport everybody is talking about the threat of fog or the need to de-ice the wings of our plane. Twice on one journey westwards we Bennetts found ourselves delayed: first in Chicago by sleet, and again, a day or two later, by fog in Los Angeles.

Nor is land-travel any freer from the hazards of inclement weather. Four times (or is it five?) we have visited Scotland hoping for blue skies and wonderful photography. But each time, out of fourteen days we have enjoyed only three or four without rain or that fine, but very wet Scottish mist.

But to return to the inconsistencies of our local weather. Most of us, let's admit it, would feel cheated if the weather continued constant day after day, month after month. Most of us rejoice in the changing of the seasons here in our true north, strong and free. Quite apart from the pleasure we feel in being able to talk about it, the unpredictability of the weather adds the spice of surprise. In fact, we should feel a genuine sympathy for those people on our planet who must always slosh through floods of water or shrink away from torrid sun; who never have the fun of making footprints in the soft, new-fallen snow; or of rustling through fallen leaves when walking in the autumn woods.

And now, as April comes again, we can look up hopefully each morning for signs of swelling buds; and listen for the cheery-ups of the robins; can raise our noses to savour sniff after sniff of the moist earthy air. However, it might be a good idea not to get carried away too soon into a cloud cuckoo-land, but remember that wise, old saying: *Ne'er shed a clout till May is out!*

She'd only give it away

Some people are born givers, not takers, and my mother was one of those, constantly handing out things and money if she saw a need. Or she was busy sewing articles (notably little girls' dresses and little boys' shirts and pants) to put into bundles going overseas or up north. Or she was organizing a small, yearly bazaar held right in our home so that a group of us teenagers could raise money to support a child in India. Then she was promoting bake sales in the park for Red Cross (that was during World War One). In fact, she was tireless in her active, generous charity. It was her oldest son, my brother Harold (himself naturally generous and usually wise) who made the rather foolish remark that I've quoted for the heading. The occasion was my mother's birthday when her children were discussing what gifts we might give her.

Someone had suggested money to spend as she wished — on a house plant, perhaps, or a new sweater, something she'd choose for herself. Previously we children had done the choosing, and so this was a real departure for us; and it was Harold who protested: "She'd only give it away!", which was indeed more than likely.

But could anyone have paid her a more spontaneous, finer tribute? I have no recollection as to what followed on that particular occasion, but the memory of it, the truth of it, the delight of it has stayed with me now for many decades. My mother and brother have long since died, but this almost accidental tribute to her has lived brightly on. "She'd give it away!"

While many people, in her place, would immediately have had self-turned thoughts in mind, not my mother! To her such a windfall was another chance to come to someone's rescue financially (our cleaning woman, with her young family, for instance). Perhaps it would mean a larger donation to the church, or an extra money order to relatives back home in England. Always it was with her an instinct and joy to "share the wealth."

So not surprisingly it was through my mother that I first appreciated the rightness of medicare where no one should lack health care, while all of us shared its cost.

Another trait in my mother's character was probably not quite so readily loved and admired. This was her sense of decorum! Having looked up that old-fashioned word in the dictionary, I find that it gives, as synonyms, expressions like good taste, seemliness, and propriety in behaviour and dress. My mother was by birth and breeding a "lady" and it made no difference to her when she exchanged a genteel style of life in England for the rough-and-tumble of the pioneer West in the early 1900s.

It was truly a lesson in etiquette to see how visitors to our home were always received and treated as honoured guests. Anything like unruliness or discourtesy among us children was firmly reproved. I fancy that we were even at times reminded to behave like "ladies and gentlemen." Can you imagine today's parents daring to use such words?

In conclusion, I'm noting that my dictionary also tells me that decorum (stuffy and stodgy as it may sound in contemporary ears) is actually derived from the Latin word for grace, but then who wants grace when gaucherie is so much more in style these days?

Anyway, I cherish a desperate sort of hope-against-hope that there may be a return to decorum and grace in the 21st century even though I and many of my fellow-hopers may no longer be here to rejoice and enjoy it.

About Noah and the Ark

For some reason, which I myself don't quite understand, I find the story of Noah and his ark slightly comical. Of course, when taken as history and recounted as such in the Bible, it's not in the least funny, nevertheless, I find it so.

Perhaps I can trace my feelings back to childhood days when I was given a Noah's ark for a Christmas present, and was both delighted and amused by all the little wooden pieces, people and animals. They certainly were entertaining, rather than historical or Biblical, so far as I was concerned.

Somewhat later, in fact, at college, I came upon a sort of "morality," written by a minor Elizabethan playwright who retold the story with an eye to amusing the groundlings in the pit.

He inserted a quite comical interlude, if I remember rightly, about how Noah's wife held up proceedings by stubbornly refusing to go onboard. I've forgotten her reasons, but if she was allergic to furs, feathers and hairs she had plenty of them to complain about.

I'm not too sure where I go on from here, but perhaps it's to recall and consider all the recent TV coverage about the dinosaurs and their disappearance from the earth. It's truly mind-boggling to think of getting a pair of them into the ark, no matter how divinely ordained!

And, of course, there were dozens of their species to house — if my toy was anything to go by. And, moreover, as a child of our Prairie West, I was puzzled that Noah (or the makers of my game) hadn't seen fit to include the coyotes and gophers.

In some cases the pairs on board (just think of the rabbits) must have propagated themselves in a big way, threatening thereby to sink the ship before it was grounded. It's not recorded as to whether there were any losses during the 40 days (?) onboard, owing to overcrowding and under-nourishment, for instance, but such details are considered irrelevant when a good story is being told. We're happy to learn that one of the doves was well enough to reconnoiter and bring back reports to Noah.

But here arises a question: Did Noah and his sons, etc., really think themselves so virtuous that they could propagate a sinless world? Well we'll give them the benefit of the doubt and make no accusations.

However, now at the end of another century, I feel sad and badly disappointed because it's so obvious that our human race (if not the animals) has been very careless about making the best of any other second chances it may have been given to amend its ways.

A child's delight in a colourful toy, and a childish faith in the good sense and goodwill of the world— that's why the reality of things can hit us hard. So we'd like to think that Noah was just the first of many who would rise to the occasion, build a timely ark, and save the planet for generations yet to come.

Noah may have been over-optimistic about his children and the dinosaurs, but he deserves full marks for his immediate response to a heavenly warning. Now it's up to us to do likewise in our own times.

The music of the spheres

It seems that in December we have more music and more kinds of music than at any other time of the year. It isn't just those carols, which we hear in hospitals, in churches, and even in shopping plazas. Everywhere there's a feeling of harmony which does, indeed, express itself in those simple, familiar songs, but which also rises into the grandeur of a Hallelujah Chorus. The universality of the Christmas theme, that is to say, the coming of peace and goodwill among us, is very close to most hearts, no matter how practical and even hardened they may usually be, and it is probably the reason that music and Christmas are so inextricably bound together.

In times of deep feeling we humans seem to turn by instinct to poetry and music. We find that nothing else can so adequately express the depths and heights of our emotions, and of our thoughts and aspirations, too. All the lullabies sung by mothers everywhere, the joyous recurrent salutations of the dawns throughout human history, the strong affirmations of hope and faith — all thus find their place in the music which we share together in December.

There seems to be something in the atmosphere these pre-Christmas days which shuns the cacophony and stridency of most popular music. Somehow, the violent emotions which are expressed by agitated, almost hysterical singers and players don't seem appropriate as an expression of the hope we have when we contemplate the coming of love incarnate into our troubled world.

I hasten to add that I find nothing really objectionable in loud and dissonant music. Life, we all agree, would be very dull if everything were always kept quiet and euphonious. But surely it must remain as a fundamental principle of civilization that loudness and dissonance must constantly be resolved into harmony.

It was Shakespeare who wrote so feelingly about the music of the spheres, of the harmony which thrills throughout the planets and the stars; a music, he added, which earthlings cannot hear because we are clothed in this "muddy vesture of decay", our mortality. But even though we cannot yet enjoy such transcendent harmonies, we can join in the more humble ones of this Christmas season.

Now that strings of coloured lights are transforming many a dark street into a veritable fairyland, it's time to say a few words of appreciation to those energetic and thoughtful townspeople who manage to put them into place. Perhaps the big tree at the bottom of Manitoba Street deserves to be mentioned first and foremost. It has already cheered so many hearts that any labour and expense involved have, I'm sure, been richly repaid. But its special splendour shouldn't make us forgetful of all the small displays which greet us at every turn. They sparkle cheerfully and warmly, telling us in yet another way that Bracebridge people like to add an extra glow to the lives of their neighbours.

I have a special place in my heart for lights of all sorts: candles, lamps, floods and spots — you name it!

Yet, after recognizing and enjoying these various little lights, it is all the more seemly to raise our eyes to the great ones, the stars, the moon, and the sun. Most of all, to the sun which gives not only light but life itself to our planet! And as a concluding thought: Whenever I gaze up at the silver radiance of the moon, I am surprised into remembering that its light is, in fact, only a reflection of the sun; and then I am reminded that the light which shines in faces of good men and women is indeed the reflection from the source of all light, the love of our planet and everyone on it.

White for Christmas

Whenever I'm shopping in the A&P store, I make a point of pausing in front of its display of plants, looking out for a possible bargain. Last week one of several pots of white cyclamens caught my eye, and immediately appealed to my sympathies. It looked so fragile, lonely, and yet so significant that I decided to take it home, and cherish it, and think about it.

After a day or so spent on the kitchen window sill it seemed to be feeling a bit chilled and sad, and so I moved it to a warmer spot hoping to coax it into a happier state. To my great relief and delight, it responded immediately; petals unfurled in creamy-white whorls and before long I was counting nine lovely blossoms rising in a gleaming cluster rather like a white-gowned corps-de-ballet in a Christmas pantomime. That made me think about the place of whiteness in nature and the arts.

Of course, there isn't such a colour as pure white except in theory. These cyclamen flowers for instance, are tinged with a faint flush of pinkish-mauve. In fact, it's this delicate blending of all sorts of colours on a white base which fascinates the observant eye. To give another example of such subtle colouring, think how the very whitest snow takes on the changing hues of the sky, how each fold is shadowed with violet, and each slight rise is barred with pale gold.

When we Northerners dream about that much-sung-about "White Christmas", it's for a fresh fall of snow that we're hoping. But on second, longer thoughts, isn't it almost as natural for us to dream about a little Lord Jesus wrapped in swaddling clothes of simple white? Surrounded, perhaps, by woolly white sheep and lambs? Plus a silvery dove or two, perched on the stable rafters? If we allow the shepherds their homespun brown and the magi their princely purple, for the sake of contrast, we still return with delight and awe to the pure white light shining in the manger.

Our North American world has decided upon the bright red of the poinsettias as a way of decorating our homes, shops, and churches at Christmas. This, I think, is because we want to put on a "merry" face for our festivities. The addition of greenery, too, is part of our desire to express the "evergreen" concept of the Christmas story. But to me these bright, warm colours are only secondary, showing our human dependence upon something close to our familiar, workaday world, while, at the same time, admitting that that white light, in its unbroken splendour, is more than our weak eyes and spirits can bear. The seven vivid colours of the spectrum are exciting, but a shaft of pure, white light is more than exciting, it's awesome.

Happy memories of Thel

Only occasionally does one read about sisters and/or brothers who have maintained through the years a close attachment one with the other. Yet such a rapport is often the happy state of affairs — as it was with my sister and me for years, and years, and years! It's not inappropriate, then, to reminisce a little about some of the joys we shared now that she is no longer here in the flesh.

Thel and I grew up together out west in Calgary, but during the earlier years, as school girls, she was more my guardian than companion. However, when we both reached our later teens, the three years difference in our ages presented no difficulties at all. Then we began a long and happy association that took us into sports together, like swimming, boating, and tennis as well as into choirs and shows of many different sorts.

But probably it was our common love of all kinds of music which began first and ended last. Together we sang in choirs and choruses, practised songs and anthems, and later did some composing. We joined our talents to compose lyrics and musical settings in such pieces as the "Little Christmas Cantata" for the Seniors' Glee Club (when Thel was pianist and I its director). Then we'd often laugh together (or groan in exasperation) when the music and words worked out smoothly (or stubbornly refused to do so!).

Playing tennis or badminton together was something rather different since sports required a less personal relationship as one concentrates on the game. But coming and going to matches, stopping for an ice-cream or a luncheon en route afforded us many comradely interludes.

Then, of course, travelling always brought us close together since hotel rooms, ships' cabins, even the back or front seat of cars would find us sharing our impressions and laughing over incidents en route. Hiking together was always one of the activities we shared with real joy, mostly in the Old Countries, England, Scotland, and Ireland, but also in faraway places — recently for instances, in Malta and the Channel Islands.

Going to theatres and concerts was also a shared delight, taking us regularly to Massey Hall, or the Royal Alex in Toronto, and frequently to Stratford, as well as to more exotic shows in Africa, Asia, and South America. Happily, neither of us was easily disappointed in a program, whether close to home in Gravenhurst's Opera House, or for example in Moscow's Bolshoi. Always we shared, too, the pleasures of anticipation and those of recollection and reflection afterwards.

Well, I see that I've already written at some length, and so must find a way of ending; but here I hesitate between the joy of giving our slideshows, or of watching the birds! If I settle for the birds, then it comes right to our own back garden here in Bracebridge where for almost 30 years we've watched together a hundred different feathered visitors, calling one another to the window, grabbing binoculars, enthusing and laughing as grosbeaks have come in gorgeous battalions, gentle doves descended and fed with rosy-grey dignity, and our all-time favourites, the chickadees, have brought almost daily, their cheerful greeting.

Undoubtedly, happiness comes to each of us in many different ways, but, perhaps, the best comes in the company of a sister like Thel.

Inventions or simply discoveries?

Doubtless we'd all like to believe that at least a few of us are capable of creating something – something previously unknown here on earth.

We honour, almost revere the inventors of the past, and hope for more to come. But in this article I'm suggesting that it's been discovery rather than invention which has brought us from a primitive way of life to a more sophisticated one.

I'm not stating as a fact that man appeared on earth only after everything else had already been put in place to satisfy his needs and desires. That would indeed be presumptuous. But the more I think about it, the more it seems probable.

Let's say that we've been given the necessary raw materials and tools – earth, water, fire, electricity (and much more) and have been invited, perhaps challenged, to develop them to their furthest limit. Our "Garden of Eden," this small planet, is to be tended and kept; and I would add, is to be extended as far as man's wit and wisdom can take it!

When I set out to give examples and proofs, I'm very conscious of my own lack of knowledge. For instance we've often been told that the wheel was one of man's earliest and most important "inventions".

But having seen round (and rounded) stones on many an archaeological site (e.g. Malta), I'm convinced that those early movers of heavy loads had already "discovered" the advantages of a rounded base rather than a flat one in order to minimize friction.

And so the immense monoliths at Stonehenge, as just one example, were transported and raised to the glory of the gods.

And what about Sir Isaac Newton and his law of gravity? Wasn't that based on his noting how things always fall to earth? So his scientific formulation was really a discovery, not an invention. But perhaps I've got slightly off-track, and so I'll move into our 19th Century and cite James Watt and his famous steam engine.

It was steam power which turned Britian's factories into mass producers of exportable goods, carried to markets around the world on rails and in ships, all of them empowered by steam. Yet, as I read history, Watt, having observed the power of steam (as it lifted the lid of a kettle) merely applied it in a big way.

But even this was after some cave man, millennia earlier, had noted it coming from a fissure in the earth and seen it rising from a pot of boiling water. However, it's only fair to grant James Watt his quantum leap in realizing how steam could be mightily harnessed.

But could it be rightly maintained that the world's languages, spoken and written, are indeed inventions rather their discoveries? Who knows how long the animals have grunted, the birds sung their songs?

Anyway, at some significant point in time, man undertook to work out his own forms of communication, and so the languages of business and literature came into being.

Which brings us, finally, to the question as to whether poets (and artists of every sort) aren't the only true inventors, co-creating with nature, all that we know of beauty and truth on earth.

The numbers game

Two's company,
Three's a crowd
And four on the sidewalk
Is not allowed.

So how about going singly, or altogether? It's an interesting numbers game that I'm playing and writing about this week.

First then, when and why does "two" form the perfect number in a human relationship? I'm sure you're all ready with good answer to that proposition.

Certainly no one wants a third to barge in on a pair of lovers, not even one's closest friend, let alone a kid brother and much less still, one's future mother-in-law!

And just as unwelcome, I'd assume, is the third who crashes the party when two happy gossips are tearing to pieces a local reputation. And, yet again, there's surely no place in the confessional for a third pair of ears.

But now we'll move along to the next number in our jingle, namely; "Three's a crowd." Well, already in the previous paragraph, I've pointed out several ways and places in which an unwelcome third has been told to get lost.

Yet, on the other hand, I've known occasions when the arrival of a third has brought great relief. A timely knock on the door, a head popped around a corner, has come like a dispensation from heaven itself.

Many an embarrassing or heated exchange between an incensed two has been cooled and ended by the advent of a diplomatic third. And then, too, when a threesome goes travelling together, it's always pleasantly possible for them to split off into a congenial pair while your single individualist goes on his or her own separate way.

As for the "four on the sidewalk" not being allowed surely that's a matter of common courtesy, not of laws enforced or ignored?

Definitely, there are times and places where four is the accepted and even necessary number, as in most card games. Moreover, many golfers prefer to make up a foursome, as also do couples who go on cruises, since men and women can then gravitate to each other and enjoy a bit of essentially masculine or feminine chit-chat.

But having dealt so far with the numbers included in our rhyme (namely, two, three and four), I think it's only fair to consider now the unit one, and the indefinite many, that's to say, the crowd, whether organized or spontaneous.

It's not difficult for most of us to sympathize with a Greta Garbo who wants "to be alone" since even the most gregarious person feels a need at times to escape from the company of others.

Similarly, or quite otherwise, most of us also enjoy being part of a cheering, clapping crowd, say, while watching a hockey final, or a July 1 fireworks display, occasions when the exhilaration seems to vary directly with the numbers participating.

So, to sum things up, it's fair to say, I think, that we've been given the choice of living alone (and liking it) or of taking our place as a small but distinct entity within the world's millions and billions, free to play out life's big game as variously and joyously as we choose.

I encounter St. Peter

This meeting with St. Peter did not come as a complete surprise. Sometime in my youth, probably back in Sunday School days, I had heard that he'd been entrusted with the keys into the heavenly places, and I'd visualized him standing on guard at the gate with a great bunch of them jingling in his hands or dangling from his belt.

Thus I was prepared ahead of time for some stiff questions, but had reasoned that if others could pass the saint's tests, probably so could I. Anyway, I was ready to put my case vigorously, and without undue modesty, St. Peter notwithstanding.

"Good morning," I cheerfully greeted the guardian figure. "I've just arrived," I added, rather unnecessarily.

St. Peter brought his gaze down from surveying the antics of a couple of exuberant cherubs who were swinging on a chandelier of stars.

"Oh, you've come already!" he exclaimed. "I thought you were planning to outlast Methuselah, and it turns out that you've barely reached your first one hundred. A bit of a quitter, eh?"

Well, that got my dander up, but I held on tight to whatever Christian humility I could summon and answered meekly (for me, that is).

"You see, sir," I said, "the streets down there in Bracebridge are rough and tough on old feet (though it's really a fine town to live in), and I decided that the jasper ones up here might be smoother and sweeter."

"Now," warned Peter, "don't begin declaring your assets before we've checked your liabilities. Where's that recording angel?" he shouted. "Ah, there you are! So with what good deeds is she accredited? How about feeding the hungry?"

Here I spoke up quickly in my own defence: "Sir, I put several tins of stew into the Food Bank last week, though I confess to having neglected it during the summer."

"Tut, tut," scolded the saint, "a shocking lapse in dependability!"

"But," I protested, in a bit of a huff," I understand from the Bible that you weren't all that dependable yourself, Peter, and were very lucky or blessed to be forgiven."

For a moment St. Peter had the grace to look shame-faced, but then he rallied and replied, "That was when I was still young and weak, before I was recognized as The Rock."

"Moreover," I pressed home my point, "you had the timely crowing of that rooster to bring you up to scratch."

"Don't rub it in!" protested Peter in his turn. "Let bygones be bygones!"

"I couldn't agree more," I thankfully rejoined, "So what extenuating circumstances can you find for me?"

St. Peter consulted the list again, pursed his lips, and shook his head. "Not so good but not so bad either," he pontificated. "I'll let you come in under certain conditions." He scrutinized me doubtfully.

"Yes?" I said, not too sure where this was tending.

"I know there's no harm in it," he went on, "no malice in their merriment, and I know that I should learn to take it in good part, but..." And here the saint shuffled his feet like any schoolboy. "Well, I don't want you telling those bright eyed, young seraphim any fishy stories about my past."